Glimpses of Life After Death

A Collection of hadith on the Transition
From this Life to the Hereafter,
The Entrance to the Garden or the Fire

Compiled and Edited by
Alpha Mahmoud Bah

Ta-Ha Publishers Ltd.
1 Wynne Road,
London SW9 0BB
UK

Published Rajab 1422/October 2001 by:
Ta-Ha Publishers Ltd.
1 Wynne Road
London SW9 0BB
Website: http://www.taha.co.uk
Email: sales@taha.co.uk

By: Alpha Mahmoud Bah
General Editor: Afsar Siddiqui
Edited by: Abdassamad Clarke

British Library Cataloguing in Publication Data
Bah, Alpha Mahmoud
Glimpses of Life After Death
I. Title

ISBN 1 842000 30 6

Typeset by: Bookwright
Website: http://www.bogvaerker.dk/Bookwright
Email: bookwright@bogvaerker.dk

Printed and bound by: Deluxe Printers,
London NW10 7NR
Email: de-luxe@talk21.com

Qur'an

That Day people will emerge segregated to see the results of their actions. Whoever does an atom's weight of good will see it. Whoever does an atom's weight of evil will see it. Qur'an 99:6-9

As for those who are kafir and die kuffar, the whole earth filled with gold would not be accepted from any of them if they were to offer it as a ransom. They will have a painful punishment. They will have no helpers. Qur'an 3:91

...whereas those who have iman and do right actions, such people are the Companions of the Garden, remaining in it timelessly, for ever. Qur'an 2:81

It is not devoutness to turn your faces to the East or to the West. Rather, those with true devoutness are those who have iman in Allah and the Last Day, the Angels, the Book and the Prophets, and who, despite their love for it, give away their wealth to their relatives and to orphans and the very poor, and to travellers and beggars and to set slaves free, and who establish salat and pay zakat; those who honour their contracts when they make them, and are steadfast in poverty and illness and in battle. Those are the people who are true. They are the people who have taqwa. Qur'an 2:177

Translation: Abdalhaqq and Aisha Bewley

Foreword

This book is for those who have come to realise that life is a journey to one certain destination, and wisely seek the knowledge necessary to arrive thoroughly prepared, with provision in hand for what lies beyond. The Final Messenger, Muhammad ﷺ has left us a wealth of instructions on this subject, and in compiling this selection, Dr. Bah has made the essential hadith directly accessible to non-Arabic speakers, especially those who have recently discovered the teachings of Islam.

In this selfless presentation, Dr. Bah has stepped aside and allowed the hadith to speak for themselves. Readers may find themselves deeply moved, as if actually in the presence of the inspiring men and women whose example we humbly imitate, sharing their grief at the death of their loved ones, may Allah be pleased with them.

Abd un-Nur Anthony Brewer
Director, English Department
Osaka College of Foreign Languages, Japan

Preface

Praise be to Allah, the Lord of the Universe, Who created the Garden and the Fire. Believing in Him, the Compassionate, the Merciful, and believing in His angels, His books, His messengers, the Day of Judgement, and the Decree, I bear witness that there is no god but Him. Whomsoever He guides there is none to mislead, and whomsoever He permits to go astray there is none to guide. May peace and blessings be upon His Noble Prophet, Muhammad - who clarified the ways to the Garden and the Fire by conveying the divine guidance to mankind and by setting the ideal example with his life - as well as his family, his companions, and all their followers on the right path until the Day of Rising.

The compiling of this book started on a most fortuitous occasion in April 2000, by the will of the Almighty. I was working on a different project about the Day of Judgement and needed detailed information from the hadith. No sooner had I consulted a few sources than I found myself with an incredibly large number of hadith on the topic. There was no way for me to use the information without systematically processing it. As I started the work, it occurred to me that a comprehensive and distilled compilation might benefit other researchers engaged in the subject, Muslim and non-Muslim alike. I also realized that, just like the initial project on which I had been working, this new project might stimulate the reader's awareness of death and the Final Judgement, and thereby serve an even greater purpose, as those phenomena apply to all members of society, not only researchers.

With these two objectives in mind, I suspended the original project to focus on this one, calling it *Glimpses of Life After Death* - since before meeting death, we can have only glimpses of it, never a complete view.

My contribution to this book basically consisted of retrieving the hadith from already existing translations, arranging them in chapters, and rewriting the text. This is too small compared with the workload of the early scholars who painstakingly made the initial collections of the hadith and that of the later scholars who pop popd and published them in print and on-line versions.

Early drafts of the book were reviewed by two Muslim brothers, Mr. Abd un-Nur Anthony Brewer of the Osaka College of Foreign Languages, Japan, and Dr. Shaukat Abdulrazak of Egerton University, Kenya. On behalf of Ta-Ha Publishers, Mr. Afsar Siddiqui also suggested improvements in the presentation of the hadith and advised on ways of making the work accessible to as wide an audience as possible. Thus I feel indebted to all the above. I pay homage to them and pray that Allah reward them with His pardon and the eternal bliss of the Garden.

For my little contribution to the book, which was possible only with the help of Allah, I do not desire any payment, material or immaterial, in this world. I wish for any good reward to be credited to my account in the Final Settlement that the book deals with. Meanwhile, I beg Allah's forgiveness for any mistakes that the book might contain. Such mistakes will be corrected as soon as they are located and the corrections included in future editions. Please forward your comments to the publisher or directly to me:

Alpha Mahmoud Bah
Rabi II 1421 / June 2001
Matsue, Japan
748-113 Nishikawatsu,
690-0823 Matsue.
E-mail: bah@igsonline.net.

CONTENTS

INTRODUCTION

To make the best use of this book, it is necessary to comprehend the approach followed in its compilation. Besides, for certain readers, reviewing the notion of hadith may be crucial. The lines below aim to satisfy these two requirements.

I. UNDERSTANDING THIS COMPILATION

1. Method of Compiling the hadith

Considering the objectives of the book - to provide a collection of hadith in English and to stimulate the reader's awareness of the issues covered - the compilation was based on two major criteria. First, for more convenience in use, only hadith from on-line sources and portable databases (CD-ROM) were considered, allowing direct retrieval of the text for quotations, instead of typing. Second, seeing that many changes have taken place in the Muslim community since the birth of the hadith, only hadith with wording and content likely to be understood by today's readers were examined. In all, roughly 260 pieces were selected from the many hadith found on the subject.

The search was made first on the Internet, currently the most popular and versatile medium for information dissemination. The bulk of the hadith selected were taken from the collections of Bukhari, Muslim, Malik, and Abu Dawud at the Website of MSA-USC (Muslim Students Association at the University of Southern California): <www.usc.edu/dept/MSA>. The hadith that could not be found on the Internet were taken from the *Mishkat* collection on the Islamic

Scholar CD-ROM, developed by Par Excellence Computers (Johannesburg, South Africa). However, the authenticity of the selected hadith is not discussed in this book, which is rather a general work.

The collection is organized into seven chapters arranged in three parts. The first three chapters discuss death and life in the grave. Chapters 4 and 5 deal with the Rising from the Dear and the processes of Judgement. Chapters 6 and 7 depict the Garden and the Fire and highlight the ways to each of them. Efforts have been made to facilitate the use of the book both as an integrated exploration and a reference work intended to provide information on specific points. Thus the chapters are divided into sections and subsections with short introductions summarising their contents. In addition, the essential teaching of the book is condensed in a separate section, the Summary. Furthermore, the hadith, which are numbered consecutively throughout the book, are listed with short descriptions permitting the reader to grasp the specific content of each hadith at a glance.

2. Rewriting the Existing Translations
The rewriting of the text was made upon permission issued in writing by Mr. Zakaria Shaikh for MSA-USC and Mr. Ahmed Asmal for Par Excellence Computers. The original translations were authored by different scholars, including the following five:

M. Muhsin Khan (*Sahih Bukhari*)

Abdul Hamid Siddiqui (*Sahih Muslim*)

Ahmad Hasan (*Sunan Abu Dawud*)

A'isha Abdarahman al-Tarjumana Bewley and Ya'qub Johnson (Malik's *Muwatta*)

Besides creating uniformity and consistency in the text, the major features of the current version reside in the handling of the Arabic terms and the approach to concision and readability. Since the compilation is essentially intended for English readers, non-English terms are avoided as much as possible. However, loanwords – words that have been naturalised and included in English dictionaries – with sound transliteration, are used like ordinary words, that is, written with the spelling of the dictionary and without italicisation. Quite a few Arabic-Islamic terms appear in the Merriam-Webster and other dictionaries, especially in the unabridged international editions.

For example, here is a list of common Arabic words used in this book that could be said to have entered the English language:

Qur'an	surah	hadith
Sunnah	salat	rak'ah
qiblah	zakat	Ramadan
hajj	hajji	jihad
Mujahid	Muhajirun	Ansar
jahiliya	salaam	houri
jinn	Shaytan	iman
shaheed	shuhada	

Dictionaries suggest several variants for some of these terms. For example, qiblah and rak'ah can be written without the final h.

When specific Arabic words are unavoidable, such as in proper names, a simplified transliteration is adopted. It must be noted that perfect pronunciation is possible only when based on the Arabic text, not on English transliterations.

As for conciseness and readability, below is a summary of the approach followed:

(1) In traditional hadith collections, it is common to encounter several versions of the same hadith. In the current compilation, however, such hadith are not repeated unless the repetition provides a significant addition; even then, instead of listing the similar hadith as a separate unit, sometimes an abstract is simply appended to the main hadith.

(2) When a hadith was found in several sources, only one source is

listed: the one offering the best wording, or simply the first consulted, in general among the on-line sources.

(3) Material that is not indispensable is omitted or summarized, and author's explanations are minimized. In general, ellipsis dots and brackets are used for such edits but if the edits do not affect the meaning, the dots and brackets are omitted. Thus, many hadith are simply introduced by the phrase 'The Prophet ﷺ said'. Nevertheless the main parts of the hadith have been preserved carefully, and virtually all the edits inside are signalled. In a few cases, the hadith are simplified and reported indirectly, without quotation marks.

(4) When a long introduction is unavoidable, or when a hadith is repeated in a different version, the main information is highlighted for the convenience of the reader.

(5) The honorific prayer for the Noble Prophet ﷺ is written thus ﷺ . For the caliphs and all other right-acting and knowledgeable Muslim (may Allah be pleased with them and grant them the Garden), this very prayer is the only occurrence for the whole book.

(6) Since gender-neutral style is gaining momentum, efforts have been made to limit using masculine generic terms. But this could not be implemented in all cases, as wordy constructions, like he/she, were also avoided. Thus, masculine elements are sometimes used in formulating general cases. Those cases should be understood as relating equally to both genders. For example, "Whoever speaks about the Qur'an on the basis of his personal opinion [alone] will find his abode in the Fire" applies to any person, whether a man or a woman.

High style was not the main concern in the current edition; accuracy and simplicity were the focus. Since the hadith are all speech transcriptions, heavily editing the text would often lead to less accuracy, while being extremely time-consuming. For that reason many parts have been left in their speech form, unrefined.

3. System of Documentation and Cross-referencing
The Bukhari hadith are referenced by volume and hadith numbers (followed by the name of the narrator or the main reporter), as the

original collection uses separate numbering by volume. The hadith from Muslim, Abu Dawud, and Malik, which are numbered consecutively throughout in the original collections, are referenced by book and hadith numbers. The other hadith, being unnumbered in the original collection used (*Mishkat*), are all referenced by the names of the collection, the transmitter, and the narrator, respectively.

This book is only a hadith compilation, not an open discussion. Therefore, although mention of the Qur'an is sporadically made, Qur'anic text was not included, except when it is part of the original hadith. Input from other scholars is not included either.

Many hadith convey more than one piece of information and could therefore be included in different sections of the book. However, each hadith is listed in only one section - where it integrates best - and cross-referencing between the sections is omitted, for the sake of concision. Hopefully the reader will easily identify such hadith and implement the cross-referencing mentally.

II. TOWARD UNDERSTANDING THE HADITH

1. Definition

Hadith, defined simply, is what has been transmitted orally and later on recorded in writing of the Prophet Muhammad's ﷺ sayings, doings, and tacit expressions of approval and disapproval. The term hadith is used in both a general sense, applying to the entire body of hadith, and the sense of a unit of the hadith, that is, a single report.

Hadith is sometimes taken to be the same as Sunnah. Yet the two terms do not always convey the same meaning. Hadith refers to the reports of the life and customs of the Prophet ﷺ and Sunnah to his actual life and customs. Under certain circumstances the two terms are sometimes used interchangeably with only a small nuance. Sometimes, however, distinguishing between the two terms is crucial: a hadith can be false - this will be discussed next - but the Sunnah itself is always true.

Hadith are classified according to parameters such as the last authority specified, the nature of the isnad (the chain of narrators) and the reliability of the reporters. The bulk of the hadith compiled in this book are traced back to the Prophet 鹿 , not to only his companions or their successors; some of them further include the words of the Almighty. The former hadith are classified as marfu' 'ascribed directly back' and the latter as qudsi 'sacred.'

2. Authenticity and authority of the hadith

The hadith were not recorded during the lifetime of the Prophet 鹿 . In fact, the Prophet has been recorded as urging some of his companions not to write anything from him except the Qur'an, and even to delete what they had already written; he ordered that his own sayings only be transmitted orally (Muslim).

But people did not limit themselves to the Prophet's 鹿 actual deeds, sayings, approvals, or expressions of disapproval. Some people even formulated reports and attributed them to him. Thus, when the scholars started recording the hadith, they experienced a great deal of difficulty in distinguishing between authentic and forged ones. Their efforts were wholly successful, yet even the hadith believed to be authentic call for some degree of caution on the whole, since they are transmitted by fallible humans of different degrees of understanding and better and worse memories.

The concerns about the authenticity of the hadith should not be exaggerated, though. Some hadith - the *mutawatir* - were transmitted by a large number of people of each generation, which makes them impossible to doubt. Many also were transmitted by dependable persons and are thereby considered sound (*sahih*).

As regards authority, once the Prophet's 鹿 order is clearly authenticated, it becomes binding upon every Muslim. This is supported by many Qur'anic ayat, such as "Whoever obeys the Prophet thereby obeys Allah ..." (4:80). Yet, this is an area in which we are dependent upon the knowledgeable people who have established whether the order was in the sense of a command or a recommendation, whether it was of a general nature or pertained only to specific situations or even certain particular people, etc. It is worth remembering that he 鹿 received revelation from the Almighty in all his teachings pertaining to the deen; thus, human being as he was, he could not be mistaken in that regard.

3. Hints for the Correct Use of the hadith

The correct use of the hadith calls for careful consideration. Alongside the critical analysis on authenticity and authority just mentioned, two points deserve particular attention. The first is distinguishing between the hadith, the Qur'an, and the contribution of the scholars, and holding each of the three at its right place. Let us consider the hadith below:

When sending Mu'adh ibn Jabal to Yemen, the Prophet ﷺ asked him: "How will you decide a case?" He replied: "I shall judge in accordance with Allah's Book." The Prophet said: "What if you do not find specific guidance in Allah's Book?" He replied: "I shall act in accordance with the Sunnah of the Messenger of Allah." The latter asked: "What if you do not find specific guidance in Allah's Book and the Sunnah of the Messenger of Allah?" He replied: "I shall do my best to form an opinion." The Prophet then patted him ... and said: "Praise be to Allah, Who has helped the messenger of the Messenger of Allah to find something that pleases the Messenger of Allah." (Abu Dawud)

It shows that in all matters the person who is to make an independent judgement (*mujtahid*) should first turn to the Qur'an, then to the Sunnah, and last to his own scholarly judgements and fatwas. His contravening this order in either direction (considering the hadith before the Qur'an or after scholarly works) would be incorrect. However, someone who is not a mujtahid ought to depend on the judgement of the knowledgeable 'ulama and fuqaha of Islam, and not try to derive his own rulings directly from the Qur'an and the hadith.

The second hint is paying attention to the essential information of the hadith, instead of the wording. Some hadith provide apparently conflicting data. For example, that "the distance between the shoulders of the unbeliever in the Fire will be a three-day journey by a swift rider" and "the thickness of his skin a three-night journey" seems difficult to grasp, considering the proportion of the human body as known to us. But, this is apparently a figure of style that simply gives an idea of the size, not exact measurements.

When used wisely, the hadith represents an invaluable source in Islam. But failure to consider the above and other important points has caused a variety of misuses. Those misuses are detrimental not only to the Muslim community, as they sometimes result in serious divergences, but also to non-Muslims, as they create scepticism about Islam.

PART ONE:

DEATH AND LIFE IN THE GRAVE

Chapter 1: Awareness of Death

Death itself is frightening. But it is made even more so by what may happen after it. As a matter of fact, it represents the bridge between this life and the next, which may be seasoned with the bliss of the Garden but may just as easily be poisoned with the eternal sufferings of the Fire. Since death is unavoidable, it is essential to increase awareness of it. This chapter offers a few hadith on the topic, arranged into two sections. The first section deals with some introductory definitions and the second with wills and recommendations.

I. INTRODUCTION

The six hadith below describe the departure of the soul from the body and its status, either in the Garden or the Fire, before the Day of Rising. The people whose souls go to the Garden will be delighted to meet their Lord. Nevertheless, one should neither anticipate nor cause one's own death. In fact, the Almighty Himself hesitates in taking the souls of the true believers, although He too loves meeting them.

1. Allah loves meeting the believers.
Bukhari 8.514: 'Ubadah ibn as-Samit

The Prophet 爨 said: "Whoever loves to meet Allah should know that Allah loves to meet him; whoever hates to meet Allah should also know that Allah hates to meet him." Someone said "But we dislike death." He explained, "It is not [as you think]: When the time of a believer's death approaches, he receives the good news of Allah's being pleased with him and His blessings upon him, and at that time nothing is dearer to him than what is in front of him. He therefore loves the meeting with Allah, and Allah too loves meeting him. But when the time of an unbeliever's death approaches, he receives the evil news of Allah's torment and His punishment, whereupon nothing is more hateful to him than what is before him. Thus, he hates the meeting with Allah, and Allah too hates meeting him."

2. Dying people see their final abode.
Muslim 40.6857: Ibn 'Umar
The Messenger of Allah 🙻 once said: "When any of you dies, he is shown his seat [in the Hereafter] morning and evening - from among the inhabitants of the Garden or the inmates of the Fire - and it will be said to him: 'That is your seat [waiting for you] until Allah raises you on the Day of Rising [and sends you to it].'"

3. The souls are received differently.
Muslim 40.6867: Abu Hurairah
The Prophet 🙻 once explained that, when the soul of a believer goes out of the body, it is received by two angels, who take it to the heavens. The dwellers of the heavens will say: "Here comes a pious soul from earth. Let there be blessings of Allah upon the body in which it resided." Then the soul is carried by the angels to its Lord, mighty is He and majestic, Who will say: "Take it to its destined end." But if the deceased is an unbeliever, as the soul leaves the body, the dwellers of the heavens say, "Here comes a dirty soul from earth." And it will be said: "Take it to its destined end." While mentioning the foul smell of the unbeliever's soul, the Prophet 🙻 covered his nose with a thin cloth that was with him.

4. Allah hesitates in taking the believers' souls.
Bukhari 8.509: Abu Hurairah
The Messenger of Allah 🙻 said, "Allah said, 'I declare war on him who shows hostility to a close friend of Mine, and the most beloved things with which My slave draws Me are what I have made obligatory for him. And he keeps on coming closer to Me through performing extra deeds till I love him. When I love him, I become his sense of hearing with which he hears, his sense of sight with which he sees, his hand

with which he grips and his leg with which he walks. Should he ask Me [for anything], I will give him and should he ask for My protection, I will protect him. I do not hesitate in doing anything as I hesitate in taking the soul of the believer, for he hates death and I hate to disappoint him.'"

5. One should not anticipate one's death.
Muslim 35.6485: Abu Hurairah
The Messenger of Allah ﷺ said: "None of you should make a request for death nor call for it before it comes, for when someone dies, he ceases [doing good] deeds; the life of a believer is only prolonged for [doing] good deeds."

6. Suicides go to the Fire.
Bukhari 2.446: Abu Hurairah
The Prophet ﷺ said: "Someone who commits suicide by throttling [himself] will keep on throttling himself in the Fire, and someone who commits suicide by stabbing himself will keep on stabbing himself in the Fire."

II. WILLS AND BEQUESTS
A. General Recommendations Muslims are urged to keep up-to-date wills [governing the settlement of debts and the third of wealth which it is permissible to bequeath, the other two-thirds of a Muslim's wealth being beyond his control and going according to the Shari'ah in algebraic proportions to close kin. Ed.]. The Prophet ﷺ, as his final bequest, mentioned the Qur'an and his family.

7. One should prepare one's testament.
Bukhari 4.1: 'Abdullah ibn 'Umar
The Messenger of Allah ﷺ said: "It is not permissible for any Muslim who has something to will to stay for two nights without having his last testament written and kept ready with him."

8. Leaving a will leads to being forgiven. *Mishkat:* Ibn Majah/ Jabir ibn Abdallah
The Messenger of Allah ﷺ said: "He who dies leaving a will has died

following a [right] path and a sunnah; he has died with taqwa and testifying to the true faith; he has died with his wrong actions forgiven."

9. The Prophet ﷺ bequeathed the Qur'an.
Bukhari 4.3: Talhah ibn Musarrif
I asked 'Abdullah ibn Abi Awfa, "Did the Messenger of Allah ﷺ make a will?" He replied, "No." I said, "How is it then that making a will is enjoined on us?" He replied, "The Prophet ﷺ bequeathed Allah's Book [the Qur'an]."

10. The Prophet ﷺ recommended the Qur'an, his Sunnah and his family.
Muwatta, Book 46, Number 46.1.3:
The Messenger of Allah ﷺ said, "I have left two matters with you. As long as you hold to them, you will not go the wrong way. They are the Book of Allah and the Sunnah of His Prophet."

Muslim 31.5920: Zayd ibn Arqam
The Messenger of Allah ﷺ once delivered a khutbah [sermon], exhorting the people thus: "...O people, I am a human being. Perhaps I am about to receive a messenger [the angel of death] from my Lord ... I am leaving among you two weighty things. One is Allah's Book, in which there is right guidance and light; so hold fast to the Book and adhere to it. The second thing is the members of my household; I remind you [of your duties] toward the members of my family..."

11. Non-Muslims can witness to Muslims' wills.
Abu Dawud 24.3598: Abu Musa al-Ash'ari
Ash-Sha'bi said: "A Muslim was about to die at Daquqa, but he did not find any Muslim to witness to his will. So he called two men of the People of the Book as witnesses. After his death, the two men came to Kufa, and, bringing his inheritance and will, they approached Abu Musa al-Ash'ari and informed him of the matter. Al-Ash'ari said: 'This is an incident the like of which happened in the time of the Messenger of Allah ﷺ ...' He made the witnesses swear by Allah after the afternoon salat that they had not misappropriated, nor told a lie, nor changed,

nor concealed, nor altered the will, and that it was the will of the man and his inheritance. He then executed the will.'"

12. A shaheed's [martyr's] will on the eve of the battle of Uhud.
Bukhari 2.434: Jabir

When the time of the Battle of Uhud approached, my father called me at night and said: "I think that I will be the first among the companions of the Prophet ﷺ to be made a shaheed. Except the Prophet's, I will not leave behind me any soul dearer to me than yours ... I owe some debt; you should repay it. Also, treat your sisters favourably."

B. RECOMMENDATIONS ABOUT FUNERALS AND BURIALS

Expressing one's desire about the rites following one's death (such as washing, shrouding, burial, and mourning) is lawful, although apparently it was not directly recommended by the Prophet ﷺ. Evidence is given below from the first two caliphs, Abu Bakr and 'Umar, and two other companions of the Prophet ﷺ.

13. Abu Bakr's will: On his using a worn out shroud.
Bukhari 2.469: Hisham's father

A'ishah said: "I went to Abu Bakr [during his fatal illness], and he asked me, 'In how many garments was the Prophet ﷺ shrouded?' I replied, 'In three pieces of white cotton cloth, and there was neither a shirt nor a turban among them.' Abu Bakr further asked, 'On which day did the Prophet ﷺ die?' I replied, 'He died on Monday.' He asked, 'What day is today?' I replied, 'Today is Monday.' He added, 'I hope I shall die some time between this morning and tonight.' Then he looked at a garment, which had some stains of saffron, and said: 'Wash this garment of mine and add two more garments and shroud me in them.' I said, 'This is worn out.' He said, 'A living person has more right to wear new clothes than a dead one; the shroud is only for the body's pus.' He died Tuesday night and was buried the same night."

14. 'Umar's will: On his burial and succession.
Bukhari 2.475: 'Amr ibn Maymun al-Awdi

I saw 'Umar ibn al-Khattab [when he was stabbed] saying, "'Abdullah ibn 'Umar! Go to the Mother of the Believers A'ishah and say, "Umar ibn al-Khattab sends his greetings to you,' and request her to allow me to be buried with my companions." So, Ibn Umar conveyed the message to A'ishah. She said, "I had the idea of having this place for myself but today I prefer 'Umar to myself [and thus allow him to be buried there]."

When 'Abdullah ibn 'Umar returned, 'Umar asked him, "What [news] do you have?" He replied, "O Amir of the Believers! She has allowed you [to be buried there]." On that 'Umar said, "Nothing was more important to me than to be buried in that place. So, when I expire, carry me there and pay my greetings to her [A'ishah] and say, "Umar ibn al-Khattab asks permission.' If she gives permission, then bury me and if she does not, then take me to the [common] graveyard of the Muslims." ['Umar further said concerning his succession to the Caliphate:] "I do not think that any person has more right to the Caliphate than those with whom the Prophet ﷺ was always pleased, till his death. And you people must obey whomever you choose after me as caliph." Then he mentioned the name of 'Uthman, 'Ali, Talhah, az-Zubayr, 'Abd ar-Rahman ibn 'Awf, and Sa'd ibn Abi Waqqas [six of the ten persons who, as mentioned in other hadith, will be admitted to the Garden].

'Umar further said "I recommend my successor to be good to the early Muhajirun, to realise their rights and protect their honour and sacred things. I also recommend him to be good to the Ansar, who, before the Muhajirun, had taken homes [in Madinah] and had adopted the Faith. He should accept the good of the righteous among them and excuse their wrongdoers. I recommend him to abide by the rules and regulations concerning the dhimmis [protectees of the People of the Book] of Allah and His Messenger, to fulfil their contracts completely, fight for them, and not to tax them beyond their capabilities."

15. Al-Harith's recommendation: On his burial.
Abu Dawud 20.3205: 'Abdullah ibn Yazid
Abu Ishaq said: "Al-Harith said in his will that 'Abdullah ibn Yazid should lead his funeral prayer. 'Abdullah did so and then put him in the grave from the side of the legs and said: 'This is how the Prophet ﷺ used to do.'"

16. 'Amr's recommendation: No female mourners.
Muslim 1.0220: 'Amr ibn al-'As

Ibn Shamasah said: "We went to 'Amr ibn al-'As, who was about to die. He wept for a long time and turned his face toward the wall, saying: '... When I die, do not let female mourners nor fire accompany me. When you bury me, fill my grave well with earth, and then stand around it for the time a camel is slaughtered and its meat distributed, so that I may enjoy your intimacy [while answering the questions asked by the angels].'"

Chapter 2: What is Done for the Dead

This chapter explains what the living should do for the dead. It consists of four sections pertaining to (1) the washing and shrouding of the dead, (2) the funeral prayer and burial, (3) paying respects to the dead, and (4) mourning.

I. WASHING AND SHROUDING

The Prophet 🕊 explained in detail the washing and shrouding of the dead. Additional elements were learned upon his demise and from narrations from his companions and suggestions by later scholars. Under normal circumstances the body should be washed once, or several times if necessary, perfumed, and shrouded in three pieces of clothing. The people who carry out the washing should preferably purify themselves beforehand. Depending on their relationships, a person of the opposite gender, such as a spouse or close family, can wash a dead person. Under circumstances such as those who die as shaheed [martyr] in battle, neither washing nor shrouding is required, as will be seen in the next subsection.

17. Making ablution before washing the dead.
Abu Dawud 20.3155: Abu Hurairah
The Messenger of Allah 🕊 said: "He who washes the dead should take a ghusl [complete washing of the body], and he who carries him should perform wudu [ablution]."

18. The best shroud.
Abu Dawud 20.3150: 'Ubadah ibn as-Samit
The Prophet ﷺ said: "The best shroud is a lower garment and one that covers the whole body; the best sacrifice is a horned ram."

19. Washing the Prophet's daughter.
Bukhari 1.168: Umm 'Atiyyah
The Prophet ﷺ, at the time of the washing of his deceased daughter, said: "Wash her from the right side to the left, starting with the parts that are washed in ablution."

20. Shrouding the Prophet's daughter.
Bukhari 2.349: Muhammad
Umm 'Atiyyah said: "One of the daughters of the Prophet ﷺ died and he came to us saying: 'Wash her three or five times - or more if you consider it necessary - with water and [the ground leaves of the tree called] sidr, and last of all put some camphor on her. When you finish, inform me.'" Umm 'Atiyyah added, "When we finished, we informed him and he gave us his waist-wrapper, saying, 'Shroud her in it.'" Umm Atiyyah is also reported to have said: "We entwined her hair in three braids."

21. Washing the Prophet ﷺ.
Abu Dawud 20.3135: A'ishah
By Allah, we did not know whether we should take off the clothes of the Prophet ﷺ, as we used to take off the clothes of our dead, or wash him with his clothes on. While the people differed among themselves, Allah cast a slumber over them until everyone had put his chin on the chest. Then a speaker spoke from a side of the house, without anyone knowing who he was: "Wash the Prophet @with his clothes on." So they stood round the Prophet ﷺ and washed him with his shirt on. They poured water on the shirt and rubbed him with it, not with their hands. A'ishah used to add: "If I had known more on this matter beforehand, none would have washed him except his wives."

22. The men who washed the Prophet ﷺ.
Abu Dawud 20.3203: 'Amir
'Ali, Fadl, and Usamah ibn Zayd washed the Prophet ﷺ, and they placed him in his grave. It was said later on that they also made 'Abd ar-Rah-

man ibn 'Awf join them. 'Ali said afterwards: "The People of the man should serve him" [i.e., the relatives of a man have both the right and the duty to take care of him].

23. Shrouding the Prophet 繠.
Abu Dawud 20.3147: 'Abdullah ibn 'Abbas
The Messenger of Allah 繠 was shrouded in three garments made in Najran, two garments and the shirt in which he died.

24. Washing Abu Bakr.
Muwatta 16.3: Yahya
Asma bint 'Umays washed Abu Bakr as-Siddiq when he died. [Before the washing], she went out and asked some of the Muhajirun who were there: "I am fasting and this is an extremely cold day. Do I have to take a ghusl [bath]?" They said, "No."

25. Washing strangers of the opposite gender.
Muwatta 16.4: Yahya
[Malik, referring to the "people of knowledge," said]: "When a woman dies and there are no women with her to wash her and no men who have the right [by marriage or blood ties to carry out the washing], she should be purified by tayammum, that is, by wiping her face and hands with [hands which have struck upon] dust." [Malik added, "When a man dies and there are only women with him, they also should purify him with dust."]

II. FUNERAL PRAYERS AND BURIALS

A. ORDINARY CASES

A supplication is normally said for the dead upon the burial. There is no specific formula, but one example from the prayer of the Prophet 繠 and another from Abu Hurairah's are shown. The funeral prayer is an obligation on the entire community but not on every individual. It may contribute to Allah's forgiving the dead person; the larger the number of participants in the prayer, the better the expected result. There is no strong objection to a believer's burying a non-believing relative, as in the case of 'Ali and his father.

26. Importance of the funeral prayer.
Abu Dawud 20.3160: Malik ibn Hubayrah

The Prophet ﷺ once said: "If a Muslim dies and [as many as] three rows of Muslims pray over him, that might assure him [admittance to the Garden]."

27. Funeral supplication by the Prophet ﷺ.
Muslim 4.2104: 'Awf ibn Malik

The Prophet ﷺ [made a funeral supplication thus]: "O Allah, forgive him, have mercy upon him, give him peace and absolve him. Receive him with honour and make his grave spacious. Wash him with water, snow, and hail. Cleanse him from faults as You would cleanse a white garment from impurity. Requite him with an abode better than his, with a family better than his family, and with a mate better than his mate. Admit him to the Garden, and protect him from the torment of the grave and from the torment of the Fire." ['Awf ibn Malik added: "I earnestly wished that I were that dead person."]

28. Funeral prayer by Abu Hurairah.
Muwatta 16.17: Yahya

Abu Hurairah was asked, "How do you pray over the dead?" He replied: "... I say 'Allahu akbar,' then I praise Allah and ask for His blessings upon the Prophet ﷺ. Afterwards I say, 'O Allah, he is Your slave and the son of Your male and female slaves. He used to testify that there is no god but You and that Muhammad is Your slave and Your Messenger - which You know best. O Allah, if he acted well, then increase the reward for his good actions, and if he acted wrongly, then overlook his wrong actions. O Allah, do not deprive us of his reward, and do not try us after him.'"

29. 'Ali burying his unbelieving father.
Abu Dawud 20.3208: 'Ali ibn Abi Talib

I said to the Prophet ﷺ: "Your old astray uncle has died." He said: "Go and bury your father, and then do not do anything until you come to me." So I went, buried him, and came back to the Prophet. He ordered me to take a ghusl and prayed for me afterward.

30. Individual prayers over the Prophet 鬃.
Muwatta 16.27: Yahya
The Messenger of Allah 鬃 died on Monday and was buried on Tuesday. People prayed over him individually, with no one leading them....

B. SHUHADA' [MARTYRS] IN JIHAD
The battle of Uhud is the one referred to in all the hadith below. Owing to the terrible circumstances - the overwhelming number of victims and the fatigue of the surviving fighters - it was permitted to shroud several bodies in one piece of cloth and bury them in one grave. No prayer was said, except for Hamzah, and, of course, no washing either, and this is the Sunnah for people who die fighting in the Way of Allah. (Incidentally, the reader is advised to learn more about the defeat of Uhud from historical records. A comparison with the overwhelming victory at the battle of Badr, a year earlier, will prove further insightful.)

31. How the Prophet 鬃 buried people killed in jihad.
Bukhari 2.431: Jabir ibn 'Abdullah
The Prophet 鬃 would shroud every two shuhada' of Uhud in one piece of cloth and then ask, "Which of them knew the Qur'an better?" When one of them was pointed out, he would put him first in the grave and say, "I am a witness for these." He ordered that they should be buried with the blood still on their bodies. Neither did he offer funeral prayer nor did he have them washed.

32. The Prophet's 鬃 prayer for Hamzah.
Abu Dawud 20.3131: Anas ibn Malik
The Prophet 鬃 did not offer prayers for any shaheed except Hamzah.

33. Several Muslims in one shroud.
Abu Dawud 20.3130: Anas ibn Malik
The Prophet 鬃 passed Hamzah, who was killed and disfigured. He said: "If Safiyyah were not grieved, I would have left him until the birds and beasts of prey would eat him, and he would be resurrected from their bellies." The garments were scanty and the slain were in great number; one, two, and three persons were shrouded in one gar-

ment. The narrator, Qutaybah, added: "They were then buried in one grave. The Messenger of Allah would ask: 'Which of them had learned more of the Qur'an?' He then would place him nearest to the qiblah."

34. Several Muslims in one grave.
Abu Dawud 20.3209: Hisham ibn Amir

The Ansar came to the Messenger of Allah ﷺ on the day of Uhud and said: "We have been afflicted with wound and fatigue; what do you command us?" He said: "Dig wide graves and bury two or three in a single grave." He was asked: "Which of them should be put first?" He replied: "The one who knew the Qur'an most." [Hisham added that his father died on that day and was buried with another victim or two in the same grave.]

35. Shuhada' are to be buried where they fall.
Abu Dawud 20.3159: Jabir ibn Abdullah

On the day of Uhud we brought the shuhada' to bury them, but the crier of the Prophet ﷺ came and said: "The Messenger of Allah has commanded you to bury the shuhada' at the places where they fell." So we took them back.

C. DEFERRED PRAYERS

The practice of the Prophet ﷺ shows that the funeral prayer can be offered after the death of a person, even for people who are far away - although some of the people of knowledge do not accept this - and it can be offered for kings and ordinary people alike. This further highlights the importance of praying for the dead.

36. Deferred prayer for an ordinary person.
Bukhari 2.339: ibn Abbas

A person whom the Prophet ﷺ used to visit died at night and was buried immediately. Informed of the event the following morning, the Prophet ﷺ asked: "What prevented you from telling me?" The people replied, "It was at night, a dark night, so we disliked to trouble you." The Prophet ﷺ went to the grave and offered a prayer.

37. Prayer for the King of the Abyssinians.
Bukhari 2.412: Abu Hurairah

The Prophet ﷺ informed the people of the death of an-Najash (King of the Abyssinians) on the day he expired. He said, "Ask Allah's forgiveness for your brother." He then made them align in rows for salat and said four takbirs.

[That king, formally a Christian, offered great hospitality to the early Muslims who fled the intolerable persecution in Makkah. He embraced Islam after the Prophet ﷺ invited him to do so in letters. Some of the people of knowledge regard this prayer as being something that the Prophet ﷺ did specially for him alone and that it is not the Sunnah and is not applicable in other cases.]

38. Deferred prayer after a longer time.
Bukhari 2.421: Abu Hurairah

A man who used to clean the Mosque died. The Prophet ﷺ, who did not know about his death, one day remembered him and asked what had happened to him. The people replied, "O Messenger of Allah! He has died." The Prophet ﷺ said, "Why did you not inform me?" The people spoke of the man slightingly. However, the Noble Prophet ﷺ said: "Show me his grave." He then went to offer a prayer.

III. RESPECTING THE DEAD

A. HONOURING THE FUNERAL PROCESSION

When applicable, walking behind the deceased to the burial - not riding or driving - is recommended, and when it is impossible to join the procession, one should stand up till it passes, irrespective of the religious affiliations of the dead.

39. Joining a funeral procession.
Bukhari 2.332: Abu Hurairah

I heard the Prophet ﷺ saying, "The rights of a Muslim on the other Muslims are that they should (1) accept his invitation, (2) reply to his sneezing, and (3) join his funeral procession."

40. Standing till the funeral procession passes.
Bukhari 2.395: 'Amir ibn Rabi'ah
The Prophet ﷺ said, "If you see a funeral procession [and is not going along with it] then stand up and remain standing till it passes you."

41. Respecting any funeral procession.
Bukhari 2.398: Jabir ibn Abdullah
A funeral procession passed in front of us and the Prophet ﷺ stood up and we with him. We then pointed out: "O Messenger of Allah, this is the funeral procession of a Jew." He said: "Whenever you see a funeral procession, you should stand up."

42. Walking, not riding, in the procession.
Abu Dawud 20.3171: Thawban
An animal was brought to the Messenger of Allah ﷺ while he was in a funeral procession. He refused to ride it. After the procession was away, the mount was brought again to him and this time he rode it. Asked about it later on, he said: "The angels were on their feet. I was not to ride while they were walking. When they went away, I rode."

43. Walking quickly in the procession.
Abu Dawud 20.3176: Abu Bakr
'Uyaynah ibn 'Abd ar-Rahman reported on the authority of his father that he attended the funeral of 'Uthman ibn Abi'l-'As. He said: "We were walking slowly. Abu Bakr then joined us and [said]: 'You saw us when we were with the Messenger of Allah ﷺ; we were walking quickly.'"

B. RESPECTING THE BODY AND THE GRAVE

Exposing or mutilating the dead is forbidden; purification is desirable for those handling the body; and one should avoid wearing shoes in a graveyard. Visiting a grave to make supplications for the dead is normal, but this reverence should not be exaggerated: prostrating before graves or building monuments over them is strictly forbidden.

44. Not to unveil a dead person's body.
Abu Dawud 20.3134: 'Ali ibn Abi Talib
The Prophet ﷺ said: "Do not unveil your thigh nor look at the thigh of either the living or the dead."

45. Not to break a dead person's bones.
Abu Dawud 20.3201: A'ishah
The Prophet ﷺ said: "Breaking a dead person's bone is like breaking it when the person was alive."

46. Not to wear shoes between graves.
Abu Dawud 20.3224: Bashir
The Prophet ﷺ once saw a man walking in shoes between the graves. He said: "Man wearing shoes! Woe to you! Take off your shoes." The man looked around and when he recognised the Prophet ﷺ he took off his shoes and threw them away.

47. Purity of the people handling the body.
Bukhari 2.374: Anas ibn Malik
We were at the burial of one of the daughters of the Prophet ﷺ and he was sitting by the side of the grave. I saw his eyes shedding tears. He said, "Is there anyone among you who did not have intercourse with his wife last night?" Abu Talhah replied in the affirmative. So the Prophet ﷺ told him to get down in the grave.

48. Visiting graves is permitted.
Abu Dawud 10.2038: Talhah ibn 'Ubaydillah
We went out along with the Messenger of Allah ﷺ , who was going to visit the graves of some shuhada'.

49. Prostrating before graves is forbidden.
Abu Dawud 11.2135: Qays ibn Sa'd
The Prophet ﷺ once told a man: "Tell me, if you were to pass my grave, would you prostrate before it?" The man said: "No." He then said: "Do not do so…"

50. Graves are not to be made places of worship.
Muslim 4.1083: Jundub
I heard the Messenger of Allah ﷺ say the following five days before his death: "…Beware of those who preceded you and used to take the graves of their prophets and righteous men as places of worship. You must not take graves as places of prostration; I forbid you to do that."

[In a similar hadith, Bukhari 2.414, A'ishah said that "the grave of the

Prophet ﷺ would have been made prominent," were it not for the fear that "it might be taken as a place for prayer."]

IV. MOURNING THE DEAD.

Mourning is natural. Weeping is permitted but wailing is detrimental to both the dead and the person who wails. Mourning implies various forms of assistance to the family of the deceased. The mourning period should not be made excessively long, though.

A. WEEPING IS PERMITTED BUT WAILING IS NOT

51. Wailing is a tradition of the days of jahiliyyah.
Bukhari 2.382: 'Abdullah
The Prophet ﷺ said, "He who slaps his cheeks, tears his clothes, and follows the ways and traditions of the days of jahiliyyah is not one of us."

52. Wailing women may be punished on the Day.
Muslim 4.2033: Abu Malik al-Ash'ari
The Prophet ﷺ said: "In my people there are four characteristics of the jahiliyyah period, which they do not abandon: boasting of high rank, reviling other people's genealogies, seeking rain by the stars, and wailing." He further said: "If the wailing woman does not repent before she dies, she will be made to stand on the Day of Rising wearing a garment of pitch and a chemise of mange."

53. Shedding tears quietly is permitted.
Bukhari 2.391: 'Abdullah ibn 'Umar
Sa'd ibn 'Ubadah became sick and the Prophet ﷺ, along with 'Abd ar-Rahman ibn 'Awf, Sa'd ibn Abi Waqqas, and 'Abdullah ibn Mas'ud visited him to enquire about his health. They found him surrounded by his household. The Prophet ﷺ asked, "Has he died?" They replied in the negative. Then the Prophet ﷺ wept. When the people saw him weeping they all wept. He said, "Will you listen? Allah does not punish for shedding tears, nor for the grief of the heart. He punishes or bestows His Mercy because of this." He pointed to his tongue and added, "The deceased is punished for the wailing of his relatives over him."

54. Not to join a procession having a wailing woman.

Mishkat: Ahmad/'Abdullah ibn 'Umar

The Messenger of Allah 鸞 forbade following a bier that is accompanied by a woman wailing shrilly.

55. Weeping on remembering the Prophet 鸞.

Muslim 31.6009: Umm Ayman

Anas reported that after the demise of the Prophet 鸞, Abu Bakr suggested to 'Umar: "Let us visit Umm Ayman, as the Messenger of Allah used to visit her." When they came to her, she wept. They asked: "What makes you weep? What is in store for the Messenger of Allah is better than this worldly life." She said: "I weep not because I am ignorant of that fact but because the revelation that used to come from the Heaven has ceased to come." This moved both Abu Bakr and Umar to tears.

B. INVOCATIONS, SACRIFICES, AND OTHER DEEDS IN FAVOUR OF THE DEAD AND THEIR FAMILIES

56. Reciting Ya-Sin over dying persons.

Abu Dawud 20.3115: Ma'qil ibn Yasar

The Prophet 鸞 once said: "Recite Surah Ya-Sin over your dying men."

57. Speaking well about the dead persons.

Abu Dawud 20.3227: Abu Hurairah

People with a bier passed by the Prophet 鸞. His companions spoke highly of the deceased person, and he said: "The Garden is certain for him." Then some people with another bier passed by. The Prophet's companions spoke very badly of him. The Prophet 鸞 said: "The Fire is certain for him." He then added: "You are witnesses for one another."

58. A dead father relieved by an offspring's sadaqah.

Muslim 13.4001: Abu Hurairah

A person said to the Messenger of Allah 鸞, "My father died and left behind property without making any will regarding it. Would he be relieved of the burden of his wrong actions if I give sadaqah on his behalf?" The Prophet 鸞 said: "Yes."

59. A child fulfilling a dead mother's vow.

Bukhari 4.23: Ibn 'Abbas

Sa'd ibn 'Ubadah consulted the Messenger of Allah ﷺ saying, "My mother died and she had an unfulfilled vow." The Prophet ﷺ said, "Fulfil it on her behalf."

60. Preparing food for a mourning family.

Abu Dawud 20.3126: 'Abdullah ibn Ja'far

The Messenger of Allah ﷺ said: "Prepare food for the family of [the deceased] Ja'far, for there came upon them an incident that has engaged them."

61. Mourning for only three days, except for husbands.

Bukhari 2.370: Zaynab bint Abi Salamah

When the news of the death of Abu Sufyan arrived from Sham, Umm Habibah on the third day asked for some perfume and scented her cheeks and forearms, saying: "No doubt, I would not be in need of this, had I not heard the Prophet ﷺ say, 'It is not legal for a woman who believes in Allah and the Last Day to mourn for more than three days for any dead person except her husband, for whom she should mourn for four months and ten days.'"

Chapter 3: Life in the Grave

This short chapter looks at the state of the dead in the grave, before the Day of Judgement. The dead are not dead, but alive: they are dead to this world but alive to the next world. Pending the Judgement, moreover, they are already receiving parts of their treatment - are in bliss or anguish.

62. The dead hear distinctly.
Muslim 40.6868: Anas ibn Malik

['Umar, mentioning the people of Badr, said that one day before the actual battle the Prophet ﷺ pointed out the places of death of the enemies participating in the battle. He would say]: "This will be the place of death of so and so tomorrow, if Allah wills." 'Umar added: "By Him Who sent him with the truth, they did not miss the places he had pointed out for them." Then they were all thrown in a well one after another, and the Messenger of Allah ﷺ went to them and said: "So and so, son of so and so; and so and so, son of so and so, have you found what Allah and His Messenger had promised you correct? I have found what Allah had promised with me to be absolutely true." Umar said: "Messenger of Allah, how are you talking to bodies without souls?" Thereupon he said: "You cannot hear more distinctly than them. [The only difference is that] they have no power to make any reply."

[According to another version of this hadith (Muslim 40.6869), the Prophet ﷺ let the corpses lie unburied for three days before ordering that they be thrown into the well. And the names mentioned included Abu Jahl ibn Hisham, Umayyah ibn Khalaf, 'Utbah ibn Rabi'ah, Shaybah ibn Rabi'ah.]

63. The dead hear the footsteps of people.
Muslim 40.6863: Anas ibn Malik

The Messenger of Allah ﷺ once said: "When the dead person is placed in the grave, he hears the sound of the footsteps [of his friends and relatives, as they walk around]."

64. The Prophet ﷺ confirmed the punishment of the grave.
Bukhari 2.164: 'Amrah bint 'Abd ar-Rahman

A Jewess came to A'ishah to ask her about something and then she said, "May Allah give you refuge from the punishment of the grave." So A'ishah asked the Messenger of Allah ﷺ , "Will people be punished in their graves?" The Prophet ﷺ asked Allah's refuge from the punishment of the grave [thus indicating an affirmative reply. On another occasion] he ordered people to seek refuge in Allah from the punishment of the grave.

65. On listening to punishment in the grave.
Muslim 40.6860: Anas

The Prophet ﷺ said, "If it were not for fear that you would abandon the practice of burying the dead, I would have certainly supplicated Allah to make you able to hear the torment of the grave."

66. The grave is the most horrible site.
Mishkat: Tirmidhi/'Uthman ibn Affan

[Once, 'Uthman] stood by the side of a grave and wept so bitterly that his beard became wet with tears. It was said to him: "You do not weep over the discussion of the Garden and the Fire, but you weep over the grave." Whereupon he reported the Messenger of Allah ﷺ as saying: "Verily the grave is the first step in the stages of the Hereafter; if someone finds salvation [at this stage] the succeeding stages become easy for him, and if someone does not find salvation in it, what follows is very hard upon him." The Messenger of Allah ﷺ is also reported as saying: "I have never seen a site more horrible than that of the grave."

Part Two:
The Resurrection
and Judgement Processes

Chapter 4: The Day of Rising

The Day of Rising, or Doomsday, coincides with the end of this world and the Final Judgement. Nobody knows for sure when the event is to take place, as mentioned in several ayat of the Qur'an, but the Prophet ﷺ indicated some of its signs. The first section of this chapter deals with those portents and the second with the terrors that accompany the event, which is often referred to as the Hour.

I. PORTENTS OF THE DOOMSDAY

Imposture, perversion, bloodshed and a variety of social unrest, as well as a huge increase of wealth, are mentioned as events that will happen before the Hour. Spiritual wealth (faith in the Allah) is also foretold; on that Day itself, however, that form of wealth will not be of any help to those who did not have it earlier.

67. When honesty is lost, wait for the Hour.
Bukhari 8.503: Abu Hurairah

The Prophet ﷺ once said, "When honesty is lost, wait for the Hour." It was asked, "How will honesty be lost, Messenger of Allah?" He said, "When authority is given to those who do not deserve it, then wait for the Hour."

68. Prevalence of ignorance, liquor, adultery...
Bukhari 1.80: Anas

The Messenger of Allah ﷺ said, "Among the signs of the Hour are the following:

1. Knowledge will be taken away [by the death of the learned people].
2. Ignorance will prevail.
3. Use of alcoholic drinks [will be common].
4. Open illegal sexual intercourse will prevail."

[In another hadith, Bukhari 1.81, instead of alcoholic drinks, the fourth item is the increase of the number of women in society and decrease of that of men, to a ratio of 1 to 50.]

69. War between two similar groups, and thirty imposters.
Bukhari 4.806: Abu Hurairah
The Prophet ﷺ once said, "The Hour will not be established till there is a war between two groups, causing a great number of casualties, though the claims [or religion, Islam] of both groups will be the same. And the Hour will not be established till there appear about thirty liars, all of whom claim to be messengers of Allah."

70. A murderer ignorant of why he murdered.
Muslim 41.6949: Abu Hurairah
The Prophet ﷺ once said: "By Him in Whose hand is my self, a time will come when the murderer will not know why he has committed murder, and the victim will not know why he has been killed."

71. Bloodshed in the Muslim community.
Muslim 41.6906: 'Amir ibn Sa'd
The Prophet ﷺ once said: "I asked my Lord three things and He has granted me two but withheld one. I begged Him that my community should not be destroyed by famine, and He granted it. I begged Him that my community should not be destroyed by drowning, and He granted it. I begged Him that there should be no bloodshed among the people of my community, but He did not grant it."

72. Tremendous increase of wealth.
Bukhari 2.493: Abu Hurairah
The Prophet ﷺ said, "The Hour will not be established till wealth increases so much so that the owner of property will be worried as to who will accept his zakat [for nobody will accept it, being not in need.]"

73. The sun rises from the west, and universal faith.
Bukhari 6.159: Abu Hurairah

The Messenger of Allah ﷺ once said, "The Hour will not be established until the sun rises from the west. And when the people see it, everyone living on the surface of the earth will have faith, although at that moment no faith 'which a self professes will be of any use to it if it did not have iman before and earn good in its iman'" [Al-An'am, 6:158].

II. TERROR OF THE EVENT

The event comes with terror, shaking everyone - as aptly described in the Qur'an, especially in its last section. All the scenes that will follow the event are also terrifying.

74. Everybody falls unconscious.
Bukhari 3.594: Abu Hurairah

A Muslim in a quarrel with a Jew said: "By Him Who gave Muhammad superiority over all the people!..." The Jew retorted, "By Him Who gave Musa superiority over all the people! ..." At that, the Muslim slapped the Jew on the face. The Jew went and complained to the Prophet ﷺ, who afterward told the Muslim: "Do not give me superiority over Musa, for on the Day of Rising all the people will fall unconscious including myself, but [when gaining consciousness, I shall] see Musa standing and holding the side of the Throne [of Allah. In fact,] I shall not know whether Musa too had fallen unconscious [and was made to get up first and I second] or was exempted from the stroke."

75. Everyone will be barefooted, naked, uncircumcised.
Muslim 40.6844: A'ishah

The Prophet ﷺ once said: "The people will be assembled on the Day of Rising barefooted, naked, and uncircumcised." I said: "Messenger of Allah, will the male and the female be together on that Day and looking at one another?" Upon this he said: "A'ishah, the matter will be too serious for them to look at one another."

76. People submerged in their own perspiration.
Muslim 40.6852: Miqdad ibn Aswad

The Prophet ﷺ once said: "On the Day of Rising, the sun will draw so close to people that there will only be a distance of one mile left ... The people will be submerged in their perspiration according to their deeds, some up to their knees, some up to the waist, and some will have a bridle of perspiration [it will be up to the mouth]."

77. Torture for evasion of zakat, a day equal to fifty thousand years.

Muslim 5.2161: Abu Hurairah

The Messenger of Allah ﷺ said: "If any owner of gold or silver does not pay the zakat due on it, on the Day of Rising, plates of fire will be beaten out for him; then they will be heated in the Fire and used to cauterise his sides, his forehead, and his back. Whenever they cool down, the process is repeated throughout a Day, the extent of which will be fifty thousand years, until judgement is pronounced upon the slaves, and he sees whether his path is to take him to the Garden or to the Fire..."

Chapter 5: The Judgement Process

Once this world has ended and all the dead have been resurrected, the Judgement will start, under the supreme authority of the One Judge: Allah, Glory be to Him. Despite the terror of the event, the most prominent feature of the judgement will be the Judge's generosity and forgiveness; in addition, there is the possibility of intercession by the Prophet Muhammad ﷺ for the believers of his community. Meanwhile, the deeds will be assessed meticulously and rewarded. The hadith that follow discuss these three factors, each in one section, and present in a fourth section some particular situations, such as cases already decided of admittance to the Garden or the Fire.

I. ALLAH'S FORGIVENESS

78. He kept 99% of His mercy for Himself.
Muslim 37.6631: Abu Hurairah

The Messenger of Allah ﷺ once said that Allah sent down one hundredth part of His mercy upon jinn, humans, and other beings on earth; it is because of this that they love one another and show kindness to one another - even the beast treats its young with affection. He has reserved for Himself ninety-nine parts of mercy, with which He will treat His slaves on the Day of Rising.

79. I am just as My slave thinks I am.
Bukhari 9.502: Abu Hurairah

The Prophet ﷺ said, "Allah says: 'I am just as My slave thinks I am, and I am with him if He remembers Me. If he remembers Me in himself, I too, remember him in Myself; if he remembers Me in a group of people, I remember him in a group that is better than theirs; if he comes one span closer to Me, I go one cubit closer to him; if he comes one cubit closer to Me, I go the distance of outstretched arms closer to him; and if he comes to Me walking, I go to him at a greater speed.'"

80. Repeated forgiveness to a repenting believer.
Muslim 37.6642: Abu Hurairah

The Prophet ﷺ said: "A slave committed a wrong action and said, 'O Allah, forgive my wrong actions,' and Allah said: 'My slave committed a wrong action and then realised that he has a Lord Who forgives wrong actions and takes to account the wrongdoer for his wrong actions.' He again committed a wrong action and said, 'My Lord, forgive my wrong action,' and Allah, exalted is He, said: 'My slave committed a wrong action and then came to realise that he has a Lord Who would forgive his wrong action or take him to account for it.' He again committed a wrong action and said: 'My Lord, forgive me for my wrong action,' and Allah said: 'My slave has committed a wrong action and then realised that he has a Lord Who forgives or punishes him for it. O slave, do what you like. I have granted you forgiveness.'"

81. He stretches out His hand by day and night.
Muslim 37.6644: Abu Musa

The Messenger of Allah ﷺ said that Allah, mighty is He and majestic, stretches out His hand during the night so that people repent for the faults committed from dawn till dusk, and He stretches out His hand during the day so that people may repent for the faults they commit between dusk and dawn, before the sun rises in the west [before Doomsday].

82. He forgives wrong actions piled up as high as the sky.
Mishkat: Tirmidhi/Anas ibn Malik

Anas heard the Prophet ﷺ saying that Allah, exalted is He, has said: "Son of Adam! Certainly I shall continue to pardon you as long as you supplicate Me and hope [for My forgiveness]; whatever your faults and wrong actions may be, I do not care. Son of Adam! even if your wrong actions pile up as high as the sky, and you ask for My forgiveness, I will forgive you. Son of Adam! if you come to Me with faults that could fill the earth and meet Me not associating anything with Me, I will come to you with forgiveness that could fill the earth."

83. One should only hope for good from Allah.
Muslim 40.6877: Jabir
I heard the Messenger of Allah ﷺ say three days before his death: "None of you should die except that he is hoping only for good from Allah."

84. Forgiving a great but fearful wrongdoer.
Muslim 37.6637: Abu Hurairah
The Messenger of Allah ﷺ said that a person who had never done any good deeds asked the members of his family to burn his body when he died and to scatter half of its ashes over the land and half in the ocean, swearing: "When Allah finds me in His grip, He will torment me with a torment with which He did not afflict anyone among the people of the world." When the man died, Allah asked him why he had made that will. He said: "My Lord, it is out of Your fear that I have done this, and You are well aware of it." Thus, Allah granted him pardon.

85. Two wrongdoers unexpectedly saved from the Fire.
Mishkat: Tirmidhi/Abu Hurairah
The Messenger of Allah ﷺ said, "Two men of those who enter the Fire will shout loudly, and the Lord, exalted is He, will say: 'Bring them out.' He will ask them why they shouted so loudly and they will reply, 'We shouted so that You might have mercy on us.' He will say, 'My mercy to you is that you should go and throw yourselves back to where you were in the Fire.' One of them will do so, and Allah will make coolness and peace for him; the other will stand still, and Allah will ask him: 'What has prevented you from throwing yourself in, as your companion did?' He will reply, 'My Lord, I hoped that You would not send me back into it after having taken me out.' Allah will then say to him, 'You will have your hope realised'. Both men will be brought into the Garden by Allah's mercy."

II. INTERCESSION OF THE PROPHET ﷺ
The intercession of the Prophet ﷺ will be direct and indirect. He will

plead in person, and the message he has transmitted to his followers (the Qur'an) will intercede - along with other specific deeds - for those who learned and used it judiciously.

86. He has reserved a special supplication for the Day.
Bukhari 8.317: Abu Hurairah
The Messenger of Allah ﷺ said: "For every prophet there is one special supplication with which he appeals to Allah, and I want to keep such an supplication to intercede for my followers in the Hereafter."

87. He received five things, one being intercession.
Bukhari 1.331: Jabir ibn Abdullah
The Prophet ﷺ said, "I have been given five things that were not given to anyone else before me:

1. Allah made me victorious by terror [by His frightening my enemies] for a distance of one month's journey.

2. The earth has been made for me a place for praying and a thing to use in performing purification [tayammum] - therefore anyone of my followers can pray wherever the time of a prayer is due.

3. The booty has been made lawful for me.

4. I have been given the right of intercession.

5. Every prophet used to be sent to his nation only, but I have been sent to the whole of humankind."

88. He will intercede after other prophets fail.
Bukhari 6.3: Anas
The Prophet ﷺ said: "The believers will gather on the Day of Rising and say: 'Should we not ask someone to intercede for us with our Lord?' So they will come to Adam and say: 'You are the Father of mankind; Allah created you with His hand; He made His angels bow down to you and He taught you the names of everything; could you intercede for us with your Lord?' Adam will say: 'I am not in a position [to do that],' and, mentioning his wrongdoing, he will feel ashamed and say: 'Go to Nuh, for he is the first messenger that Allah sent to the inhabitants of the earth.'

"Thus they will come to Nuh and he will say: 'I am not in a position [to do that],' and, mentioning his having requested something of his Lord about which he had no [proper] knowledge [Hud, 11:45-46], he will feel ashamed and say: 'Go to the Friend of the Merciful [Ibrahim].'

"Therefore they will come to Ibrahim, who will say: 'I am not in a position to do that.' Go to Musa, the slave to whom Allah talked and to whom He gave the Torah. So they will come to Musa and he will say: 'I am not in a position to do that,' and, mentioning the taking of another person's life [Al-Qasas, 28:15-16], he will feel ashamed in the sight of his Lord and will say: 'Go to 'Isa, Allah's slave and messenger, Allah's word and spirit.'

"They will therefore come to 'Isa; but he will say: 'I am not in a position to do that. Go to Muhammad, the slave whom Allah has forgiven for all his wrongdoings, past and future.'

"Thus they will come to me and I will set forth to ask permission to come to my Lord, and permission will be given. When I then see my Lord, I will prostrate. He will leave me thus for such time as it pleases Him, and then it will be said: 'Raise your head. Ask and it will be granted. Speak and it will be heard. Intercede and your intercession will be accepted.' So I will raise my head and praise Him with a form of praise that He will teach me. Then I will intercede and He will set a limit [as to the number of people] to admit into the Garden.

"Afterward I will return to Him and bow down as before. I will intercede and He will set another limit. Then I will return for a third time, then a fourth, and I shall say: 'There remain in the Fire only those whom the Qur'an has confined and who must be there for eternity. There shall come out of the Fire any who has said 'There is no god but Allah' and who has in his heart goodness weighing a barley-corn; then anyone who has said, 'There is no god but Allah' and who has in his heart goodness weighing a grain of wheat; and finally anyone who has said, 'There is no god but Allah' and who has in his heart goodness the weight of the tiniest ant.'"

89. The luckiest person is anyone who benefits from his intercession.

Bukhari 1.98: Abu Hurairah

I said: "Messenger of Allah! Who will be the luckiest person, who will gain your intercession on the Day of Rising?" He said: "Abu Hurairah, I have thought that none would ask me about that before you, as I know your longing for hadith. The luckiest person who will have my intercession on the Day of Rising will be the one who has said sincerely from the bottom of his heart 'There is no god but Allah.'"

90. He will plead that Abu Talib be in the shallowest part of the Fire.

Muslim 1.0408: 'Abbas ibn 'Abd al-Muttalib

The Prophet ﷺ was asked: "Have you benefited Abu Talib in any way [because he defended you fervently]?" He replied: "Yes. He may be in the shallowest part of the Fire, though for me this would be as if he were in the deepest part of it."

91. Intercession through the Qur'an.

Muslim 4.1757: Abu Umamah

The Messenger of Allah ﷺ said: "Recite the Qur'an, for on the Day of Rising it will come as an intercessor for those who recite it. Recite the two bright ones, Surahs al-Baqarah and Al 'Imran, for on the Day of Rising they will come as two clouds or two shades, or two flocks of birds in ranks, pleading for those who recited them. Recite al-Baqarah, for to take recourse to it is a blessing and to give it up is a cause of grief, and magicians cannot confront it."

92. Intercession through fasting and the Qur'an.

Mishkat: Bayhaqi/'Abdullah ibn 'Amr

The Messenger of Allah ﷺ said, "Fasting and the Qur'an intercede for a man. Fasting says, 'O my Lord, I have kept him away from his food and his appetites by day, so accept my intercession for him.' The Qur'an says, 'I have kept him away from sleep by night, so accept my intercession for him.' Then their intercession is accepted."

93. Intercession of reciters of the Qur'an.

Mishkat: Ahmad/'Ali ibn Abi Talib

The Prophet ﷺ said, "If anyone recites the Qur'an, learns it by heart, declares what is lawful in it to be lawful and what is unlawful in it to be unlawful, Allah will bring him into the Garden and make him the intercessor for ten of his family, all of whom had deserved the Fire."

III. EVALUATION OF DEEDS

A. SCOPE OF THE DEEDS

What deeds carry weight on the Day of Judgement and how are they weighed? After defining the deeds taken into account - those done with faith in the One, Allah - and the principle of requital in this world, the hadith below clarify the following things: the best deeds are those done regularly, even if they appear small; some specific deeds keep on yielding fruit after the death of the persons who performed them; and no one knows exactly the overall appreciation of his or her deeds, not even the Prophet ﷺ.

94. No reward for unrepentant or unfaithful people.

Muslim 1.0416: A'ishah

I said: "Messenger of Allah, the son of Jud'an established good relationships and fed the poor. Would that be of any avail to him?" He said: "It would be of no avail to him, as he never said: 'O my Lord, pardon my wrong actions on the Day of Rising.'"

95. Expiation now, forgiveness in the Hereafter.

Bukhari 1.17: 'Ubadah ibn as-Samit

The Messenger of Allah ﷺ said while a group of his companions were around him, "Swear allegiance to me:

– Not to join anything in worship along with Allah
– Not to steal
– Not to commit illegal sexual intercourse
– Not to kill your children
– Not to accuse an innocent person
– Not to disobey when enjoined to do good deeds.

"Whoever among you fulfils his pledge will be rewarded by Allah. And whoever indulges in any of them and gets a punishment in this world will have that punishment serve for expiation. And if someone indulges in any of them and Allah conceals his wrong action, it is up to Him to forgive him or punish him [in the Hereafter]."

96. The one stoned to death enters the Garden.
Abu Dawud 38.4414: Abu Hurairah

A man of the tribe of Aslam came to the Prophet ﷺ and confessed that he had had illicit intercourse with a woman. Apparently, the Prophet ﷺ wanted to turn a deaf ear to him at first. But when the man confessed five times and insisted that he had "unlawfully done with her what a man may lawfully do with his wife," the Prophet ﷺ asked: "What do you want from what you have said?" He replied: "I want you to purify me." Thus the Prophet ﷺ gave order that the man be stoned to death, according to the law on the matter.

Afterward, the Prophet ﷺ heard one of his companions saying to another: "Look at this man whose fault was concealed by Allah but who would not leave the matter alone, so that he was stoned like a dog." The Prophet ﷺ said nothing to them but walked on for a while, till he came to the corpse of an ass with its legs in the air. He asked for the two men and told them: "Go down and eat some of this ass's corpse." They replied: "Messenger of Allah! Who can eat any of this?" He said: "The dishonour you have just shown to your late brother is more serious than eating some of this ass's corpse. By Him in Whose hand my soul is, [the man stoned to death for the crime he committed] is now among the rivers of the Garden and plunging into them."

97. The Garden is gained only out of His mercy.
Muslim 39.6770: A'ishah

The Messenger of Allah ﷺ used to say: "Observe moderation [in doing good deeds], and if you fail to observe it perfectly, try to do as much as you can [to live up to this ideal of moderation] and be happy, for none would be able to get into the Garden because of his deeds alone." The Companions of the Prophet ﷺ said: "Messenger of Allah, not even you?" He said: "Not even I, unless Allah wraps me in His mercy. And bear in mind that the deed most loved by Allah is the one that is done regularly, even if it looks insignificant."

98. At death all actions stop, except three.
Muslim 13.4005: Abu Hurairah
The Messenger of Allah ﷺ said: "When a man dies, all his acts come to an end, except for three: (1) enduring sadaqah, (2) knowledge by which people benefit, and (3) a right-acting child who prays for him."

99. Not even the Prophet ﷺ knows what waits for him.
Bukhari 2.334: Kharijah ibn Zaid ibn Thabit
Umm al-Ala', an Ansar woman who gave the pledge of allegiance to the Prophet ﷺ, said to me, "The Muhajirun were distributed among us by drawing lots and we got 'Uthman ibn Madh'un in our share. We made him stay with us in our house. Then he suffered from a disease that proved fatal. When his body was given a bath and shrouded, I said, 'May Allah be merciful to you, O Abu as-Sa'ib! I testify that Allah has honoured you.' The Prophet ﷺ who had come, said: 'How do you know that Allah has honoured him?' I replied: 'Messenger of Allah! on whom else will Allah bestow His honour?' The Prophet ﷺ said, 'I too wish him good, but by Allah, I do not know what Allah will do with me, though I am a Prophet.'"

B. WEIGHT OF THE INTENTIONS BEHIND THE DEEDS
Religious deeds can be broadly classified into two patterns, doing what is recommended and refraining from what is forbidden. The intention of doing a good deed is always taken into account and rewarded, even when the deed is not carried out. The intention in refraining from doing a bad deed is also rewarded. In general, the intentions of doing bad deeds are not accounted for when the deeds are not actually carried out, but sometimes they are.

100. The rewards for deeds depend on the intentions.
Bukhari 1.1: 'Umar ibn al-Khattab
I heard the Prophet ﷺ saying, "Actions are only by intentions, and each man has only that which he intends…"

101. More than seven hundred rewards for one good deed.
Muslim 1.0237: Ibn 'Abbas

The Prophet ﷺ once said: "Allah has written the good and bad actions, then He explained that. Whoever intends to do a good action but does not do it, Allah writes it down with Himself as a complete good action. If he intends to do it and does it, Allah writes it down with Himself as ten good actions, up to seven hundred multiples [of it], up to many multiples [of it]. If he intends to do a wrong action then does not do it, Allah writes it down with Himself as a complete good action. If he intends to do it and then does it, Allah writes it down as a single wrong action."

102. Extra salat missed but still rewarded.
Abu Dawud 5.1309: A'ishah

The Prophet ﷺ said: "If a person who regularly offers [extra salat] at night is dominated by sleep [on a certain night], he or she will still be rewarded as having performed salat that night too; the sleep will be considered as sadaqah."

103. Dying in bed but rewarded as a shaheed.
Muslim 20.4695: Sahl ibn Abi Umamah

The Messenger of Allah ﷺ said: "He who sought martyrdom with sincerity will be ranked by Allah among the shuhada', even if he died in his bed."

104. Both the murderer and the murdered to go to the Fire.
Muslim 41.6898: Ahnaf ibn Qays

The Prophet ﷺ once said: "When two Muslims confront each other with swords, both the slayer and the slain will be in Fire." It was said: "Messenger of Allah, it may be so in the case of the one who killed, but what about the one who was slain, [why would he too be sent to the Fire?]" Thereupon he said: "He too intended to kill his companion."

IV. PARTICULAR CASES

By His infinite bounty, the Almighty has already decided on the admission to the Garden of all His prophets (peace be upon them), the four Guided Caliphs, and several other people, men and women. On the other hand, He has already condemned certain individuals to the Fire. Meanwhile, some persons who think that they are lost will be admitted to the Garden, whereas some of those who expect the Garden will go to the Fire. The unexpected ending of certain cases is actually spectacular, once more highlighting the power of Allah. All the above cases are arranged in two subsections as follows:

A. PREDETERMINED ENTRANCE TO THE GARDEN AND THE FIRE

105. All the prophets are in the Garden.
Bukhari 5.721: A'ishah

When the Prophet ﷺ was in good health, he used to say, "Never does a prophet die before he is shown his place in the Garden. After seeing his place, he will be given the options [to stay alive for some more time or to die]."

106. Prophets, shuhada', and infants are in the Garden.
Abu Dawud 14.2515: Hasana'

The Prophet ﷺ once said: "Prophets are in the Garden, shuhada' are in the Garden, infants are in the Garden, and children buried alive are in the Garden."

107. Abu Bakr is in the Garden.
Abu Dawud 40.4635: Abu Hurairah

The Prophet ﷺ once said: "Jibril came to me and, taking me by the hand, he showed me the gate of the Garden by which my people will enter." Abu Bakr then said: "Messenger of Allah! I wish I were with you so that I could see it." The Prophet ﷺ then said: "You, Abu Bakr, will be the first of my people to enter the Garden."

108. The famous ten promised the Garden.
Abu Dawud 40.4632: Sa'id ibn Zayd

After a person mentioned Ali's name in a mosque, Sa'id ibn Zayd got up and declared: "I bear witness that I heard the Messenger of Allah ﷺ say: 'Ten persons will go to the Garden: [1] The Prophet ﷺ will go to the Garden, [2] Abu Bakr will go to the Garden, [3] Umar will go to the Garden, [4] 'Uthman will go to the Garden, [5] Ali will go to the

Garden, [6] Talhah will go to the Garden, [7] az-Zubayr ibn al-Awwam will go to the Garden, [8] Sa'd ibn Malik will go to the Garden, [9] 'Abd ar-Rahman ibn 'Awf will go to the Garden.' If I wish, I can mention the tenth." The People asked: "Who is he?" He kept silence. They again asked: "Who is he?" He replied: "He is [10] Sa'id ibn Zayd."

109. Ja'far flying in the Garden along with angels.
Mishkat: Tirmidhi/Abu Hurairah
The Messenger of Allah ﷺ said, "I saw Ja'far flying in the Garden along with the angels."

110. The Garden is desirous of 'Ali, 'Ammar, Salman.
Mishkat: Tirmidhi/Anas ibn Malik
The Messenger of Allah ﷺ said, "The Garden is desirous of three persons: 'Ali, 'Ammar, and Salman."

111. Khadijah, the Mother of the Believers, is in the Garden.
Muslim 31.5967: Abu Hurairah
Jibril once came to the Messenger of Allah ﷺ and said: "Messenger of Allah, Khadijah is coming to you with a vessel of seasoned food or drink. When she arrives, offer her greetings from the Exalted and Glorious and on my behalf, and give her the glad tidings of a palace of jewels in the Garden wherein there is no noise or toil."

112. Ghumaysah, daughter of Milhan, in the Garden.
Muslim 31.6011: Anas
The Messenger of Allah ﷺ said: "I entered the Garden and heard the noise of footsteps. I said: 'Who is it?' They said: 'It is Ghumaysah, daughter of Milhan, the mother of Anas ibn Malik.'"

113. Ar-Rumaysah, Bilal, 'Umar in the Garden.
Bukhari 5.28: Jabir ibn Abdullah
The Prophet ﷺ said, "I saw myself [in a dream] entering the Garden, and behold! I saw ar-Rumaysah, Abu Talhah's wife. I heard footsteps and asked, 'Who is it?' Somebody said, 'It is Bilal.' Then I saw a palace and a lady sitting in its courtyard. I asked, 'For whom is this palace?' Somebody replied, 'It is for Umar.'"

114. Fatimah in the Garden.
Bukhari 4.819: A'ishah

Once Fatimah came to us, and her gait resembled that of the Prophet
☀. The Prophet ☀ said, "Welcome, daughter!" He made her sit beside
him and told her a secret. Then she started weeping. I asked her, "Why
are you weeping?" He again told her something and she started laugh-
ing. I said, "I never saw happiness so close to sadness as I saw today." I
asked her what the Prophet ☀ had told her. She said, "I would never
disclose the secret of the Messenger of Allah." When the Prophet ☀
died, I asked her about it again. She replied: "The Prophet ☀ said:
'Every year Jibril used to revise the Qur'an with me once only, but this
year he has done so twice. I think this portends my death, and you will
be the first of my family to follow me.' So I started weeping. Then he
said. 'Don't you like to be the mistress of all the ladies of the Garden
…?' So I laughed."

115. Al-Hasan, al-Hussein in the Garden. *Mishkat*: Tirmidhi/ Hudhayfah

I asked my mother's permission to go to the Prophet ☀, perform the
sunset salat with him, and ask him to pray for our forgiveness. I went
and performed the salat along with the Prophet. He remained in salat
till he performed the night salat. Afterward, I followed him. When he
heard my voice he said, "Who is this? Is it Hudahyfah?" When I told
him that it was, he said, "What do you require? Allah forgives you and
your mother! Here is an angel who has never come down to Earth
before tonight. He asked his Lord's permission to give me a greeting
and give me the good news that Fatimah will be the chief lady among
the inhabitants of the Garden, and that al-Hasan and al-Hussein will
be the chief ones among the youth who go to the Garden."

116. 'Amr ibn Luhayy in the Fire.
Muslim 40.6838: Abu Hurairah

The Messenger of Allah ☀ is reported as saying: "I saw 'Amr ibn Luhayy
ibn Qam'a ibn Khindif, brother of Bani Ka'b, dragging his intestines in
the Fire."

B. Unexpected and Spectacular Sentences

117. Hopeless Thabit in the Garden.
Muslim 1.0214: Anas ibn Malik

When the ayah "You who have iman! do not raise your voices above the voice of the Prophet and do not be as loud when speaking to him as you are when speaking to one another, lest your actions should come to nothing without your realising it" [Al-Hujurat, 49:2-5] was revealed, Thabit ibn Qays confined himself to his house, deliberately avoiding the Prophet 鑏. The Prophet, however, asked Sa'd ibn Mu'adh about him, saying: "Abu 'Amr, how is Thabit, is he sick?" Sa'd said: "He is my neighbour, but I do not know of his being sick." Sa'd came to him and related the query of the Prophet." Thabit said: 'You know well that of us all, mine is the voice which is louder than the Prophet's, so I am one of the denizens of Fire.' Sa'd informed the Prophet 鑏 about it, but the latter observed: "[No, not so!] He is one of the dwellers of the Garden."

118. Ibrahim's father changed into a beast for the Fire.
Bukhari 4.569: Abu Hurairah

The Prophet 鑏 said, "On the Day of Rising, Ibrahim will meet his father Azar, whose face will be dark and covered with dust, and he will tell him: 'Did not I tell you not to disobey me?' His father will reply: 'Today I will not disobey you.' Ibrahim will say: 'Lord! You promised me not to disgrace me on the Day of Rising, and what will be more disgraceful to me than cursing and dishonouring my father?' Then Allah will say: 'I have forbidden the Garden for the unbelievers.' And Ibrahim will be addressed, 'Ibrahim, look! What is underneath your feet?' Ibrahim will look down and see a blood-stained animal that will be caught by the legs and thrown into the Fire."

119. A potential shaheed commits suicide and goes to the Fire.
Bukhari 5.514: Sahl ibn Sa'd as-Sa'idi

Among the companions of the Prophet 鑏 present at a certain battle, there was a man who could not help pursuing any isolated pagan to strike him with his sword. Somebody said of him, "None has benefited the Muslims today more than him." On that, the Messenger of Allah said, "Yet, he is of the people of the Fire." One man secretly followed the warrior in question, trying to ascertain the Prophet's statement. Whenever the soldier stopped he stopped with him, and whenever the soldier hastened, he hastened with him.

After some time, the "brave" soldier was wounded severely, and, seeking to die at once, he planted his sword into the ground, put its point against his chest in between his breasts, and then threw himself on it to commit suicide. On that, the man who was secretly accompanying him came to the Prophet 鐥 and said, "I testify that you are the Messenger of Allah." The Prophet 鐥 said, "What makes you say so?" He explained: "It is concerning the man whom you mentioned as one of the dwellers of the Fire. The people were surprised by your statement, and I set out to find the truth for them. So I went out after him and he was then afflicted with a severe wound and because of that, he committed suicide [and thereby condemned himself to the Fire]."

The Prophet 鐥 then said, "A person may do what looks like the deeds of the dwellers of the Garden but be of the dwellers of the Fire; another may do what looks like the deeds of the dwellers of the Fire, but be of the dwellers of the Garden."

120. A right-acting man goes to the Fire for one remark.
Abu Dawud 41.4883: Abu Hurairah
I heard the Messenger of Allah 鐥 say: "There were two men among the Children of Isra'il, one of whom would commit wrong actions while the other strove to do his best in the world. The man who exerted himself in worship always advised the other to refrain from doing wrong actions. One day, after the wrongdoer told him, 'Leave me alone with my Lord....,' he retorted: 'I swear by Allah, that Allah will not forgive you, nor will He admit you to the Garden.' When their souls were taken, however, the Lord of the worlds said to the man who had striven hard in worship: 'Had you knowledge about Me or had you power over what I have in My hand [to tell the other that I will not forgive him]?' The Almighty eventually ordered: 'Take him to the Fire.' And to the wrongdoer, He said: 'Go and enter the Garden by My mercy.'"

PART THREE:

THE GARDEN AND THE FIRE

Chapter 6: Glimpses of the Garden and the Fire

After a brief introduction, this chapter depicts the Garden and the Fire in two other sections. Like all the other hadith in this book, the hadith in this chapter offer only additional information to the Qur'an. Striking descriptions of both the Garden and the Fire are indeed available in the Book of Allah.

I. INTRODUCTION

The Garden and the Fire are already created. The Garden's inhabitants who had disagreements between themselves in this world will reconcile before their entrance. There will be no death in either place, which will increase the delight of the inhabitants of the Garden but also the grief of the inmates of the Fire.

121. Dispute between the Fire and the Garden.
Muslim 40.6818: Abu Hurairah

The Messenger of Allah ﷺ said: "There was a dispute between the Fire and the Garden and the Fire said: 'The haughty and the proud shall find their abode in me.' And the Garden said: 'The meek and the humble shall find their abode in me.' Thereupon Allah, the Exalted and Glorious [addressing the Fire] said: 'You are [the means] of My punishment, by which I punish those of My slaves whom I wish.' And [addressing the Garden] He said: 'You are only My mercy, by means of which I shall show my compassion to those whom I wish. But each of you shall be full.'"

122. The Fire will be overcrowded, but the Garden still spacious.

Muslim 40.6825: 'Abd al-Wahhab ibn 'Ata

The Prophet ﷺ said: "[After the ill-fated enter the Fire], it will continue to say: 'Are there any more,' until Allah, mighty is He and majestic, will place His foot therein and some of its parts will draw close to the others and it shall say: 'Enough, enough, by Your honour and Your dignity!' On the other hand, there shall be enough space in the Garden until Allah will make a new creation to fill it."

123. The last people to get out of the Fire.

Bukhari 8.565: Abu Said Al-Khudri

The Messenger of Allah ﷺ said, "When the people of the Garden have entered the Garden and the people of the Fire have entered the Fire, Allah will say: 'Take out of the Fire whoever has faith equal to a mustard seed in his heart.' They will come out, and by that time they would have burnt and become like coal. Then they will be thrown into a river called al-Hayat ["Life"] and they will spring up just as a seed grows on the bank of a rainwater stream."

124. No death in either the Garden or the Fire.

Muslim 40.6830: Umar ibn Muhammad

The Messenger of Allah ﷺ said: "When the inhabitants of the Garden have gone to the Garden and the inmates of the Fire have gone to the Fire, death will be called, placed between the Garden and the Fire, then slaughtered. Afterward the following announcement will be made: 'Inhabitants of the Garden! there is no more death! Inmates of the Fire! there is no more death!' This will increase the delight of the inhabitants of the Garden and the grief of the inmates of the Fire."

125. The Prophet ﷺ dreams about the Fire and the Garden.

Bukhari 2.468: Samurah ibn Jundub

After the morning salat, the Prophet ﷺ used to ask us, "Who among you had a dream last night?" One day he asked us whether anyone had seen a dream. We replied in the negative. Then he said: "I saw a dream last night, in which two men came to me, caught hold of my hands, and took me to the Sacred Land [Jerusalem]. There, I saw a person sitting and another standing with an iron hook in his hand, pushing it inside the mouth of the former till it reached the jawbone. He then tore off one side of the man's cheek, and then did the same with the other side. Meanwhile, the first side of his cheek became normal and then he repeated the same operation, again and again. I said, 'What is this?' My companions told me to proceed.

"We went on till we came to a man lying flat on his back, and another man crushing his head with a piece of rock. Whenever he struck him, the stone rolled away. The man went to pick it up and by the time he returned, the crushed head had returned to its normal state and he struck it again, and so on. I said, 'Who is this?' They told me to proceed.

"We proceeded and passed by a [huge] hole like an oven, with a narrow top and a wide bottom. A fire was kindled underneath that hole and there were naked men and women inside. Whenever the flame went up, the people were lifted up to such an extent that they were about to get out of it, and when the fire quietened, they went down into it. I said, 'Who are these?' They told me to proceed.

"So we proceeded till we reached a river of blood with a man inside. Facing him was another man standing at the bank of the river with stones in front of him. Whenever the man in the river wanted to come out, the other man threw a stone in his mouth and caused him to retreat. I asked, 'What is this?' They told me to proceed.

"We proceeded till we reached a flourishing green garden with a huge tree, near the root of which was sitting an old man and some children. Another man near the tree was kindling a fire in front of him. Then my companions made me climb up the tree to enter a house, which was better than those I have ever seen. In it were some old and young men, women and children. Then they took me out of that house and made me climb up the tree to enter another house that was better than the first, containing old and young people. I said to them, 'You have made me ramble all the night. Could you tell me all about what I have seen.'

"They then explained: 'The one whose cheek was being torn away was a liar. He used to tell lies, and the people would report those lies on his account, spreading them all over the world. So, he will be punished like that till the Day of Rising. The person whose head was being crushed is one to whom Allah had given knowledge of the Qur'an but who used to sleep at night [instead of reciting it] and who did not use to act upon it by day. So this punishment will go on till the Day of Rising. Those you saw in the hole were adulterers. And the one in the river of blood was one of the people dealing in usury [*riba*].

"'[On the other hand, my companions continued], the old man who was sitting at the base of the tree was Ibrahim, and the little children around him were the offspring of humankind; the one who was kindling the fire was Malik, the gate-keeper of the Fire. The first house that you visited was the house of the common believers and the second that of the shuhada'. I am Jibril and this is Michael. Raise your head.' I raised my head and saw a thing like a cloud over me. They said, 'That is your place.' I said, 'Let me enter my place.' They said, 'You have some life not yet completed. When you complete it you will enter your place.'"

126. Mutual retaliation before entrance to the Garden.
Bukhari 8.542: Abu Said Al-Khudri
The Messenger of Allah ﷺ said: "The believers, after being saved from the Fire, will be stopped at a bridge between the Garden and the Fire, and mutual retaliation will be established among them regarding wrongs they have committed in the world against one another. After they are cleansed and purified, they will be admitted to the Garden, and, by Him in Whose hand Muhammad's self is, everyone of them will know his dwelling in the Garden better than he knew his dwelling in this world."

II. GLIMPSES OF THE GARDEN

A. BEATITUDE OF THE INHABITANTS OF THE GARDEN
The bliss of the people of the Garden is indescribable, just as stated in the first hadith of this subsection. Alongside the nice food and drink

described in the Qur'an, the inhabitants of the Garden will be granted sound bodies, eternal youth, and even freed from the need to answer the call of nature. Interestingly enough, every aspect of enjoyment is considered, from indoor intimacies to public entertainment and outdoor relaxations. The most appreciated of all pleasures, though, will be the honour of seeing the face of Allah.

127. No soul knows what comfort is in the Garden.
Muslim 40.6780: Abu Hurairah

The Prophet ﷺ said: "Allah, exalted is He, said: 'I have prepared for My slaves what no eye has ever seen, no ear has ever heard, and has never occurred to a human heart.'" He then recited this ayah: "No self knows the delight that is hidden away for it in recompense for what it used to do." (As-Sajdah, 32:17).

128. The lowest in rank satisfy all their desires.
Muslim 1.0351: Hammam

The Messenger of Allah ﷺ explained that the lowest in rank among the inhabitants of the Garden will repeatedly be asked to formulate their desires. After they have expressed all their desires, Allah will say: "For you is granted what you desire and the like of it alongside."

129. Seeing the face of Allah.
Muslim 42.7078: Abu Hurairah

The companions of the Prophet ﷺ once asked: "Messenger of Allah, shall we be able to see our Lord on the Day of Judgement?" He said: "Do you have any difficulty in seeing the sun at noon when there is no cloud over it?" They said: "No." He continued: "Do you have any difficulty in seeing the moon on the fourteenth night when there is no cloud over it?" They said: "No." Thereupon he said: "By Allah, the One in Whose hand my self is, you will not face any more difficulty in seeing your Lord than you would in seeing the sun or the moon."

130. All inhabitants will be thirty metres tall.
Bukhari 8.246: Abu Hurairah

The Prophet ﷺ said, "Allah created Adam in his complete shape and form, sixty cubits [about 30 meters] in height.... . Whoever enters the

Garden, will be of the shape and form of Adam - which has been decreasing in his offspring continuously to the present time."

131. No need to answer the call of nature.
Bukhari 4.544: Abu Hurairah

The Messenger of Allah 變 said, "The first group of people who will enter the Garden will be glittering like the full moon, and those who will follow them will glitter like the most brilliant star in the sky. They will not answer the call of nature nor spit or have any nasal secretions. Their combs will be of gold, and their sweat will smell like musk. Aloes wood will be used in their centres. Their wives will be houris. All of them will look alike and will resemble their father Adam, sixty cubits tall."

132. All will be aged thirty or thirty-three, with no need even to shave.
Mishkat: Tirmidhi/Mu'adh ibn Jabal

The Prophet 變 said, "The inhabitants of the Garden will enter the Garden hairless, beardless [without the need to shave], with their eyes anointed with collyrium, aged thirty or thirty-three."

133. All have at least 80,000 servants and 72 wives.
Mishkat: Tirmidhi/Abu Sa'id

The Messenger of Allah 變 said, "The lowliest of the inhabitants of the Garden will be he who has eighty thousand servants, seventy-two wives, and for whom a round pavilion of pearls, chrysoprase, and rubies as large as the distance between al-Jabiyah and San'a will be set up." By the same link of narrators, he said, "Those who are to go to the Garden, who die whether young or old, will come into the Garden in their thirties and never grow older - and the same applies to those who will go to the Fire." He also said, "They will wear crowns, the smallest pearl of which will illuminate the space between the east and the west.... When a believer in the Garden wishes for [anything, the wish will be accomplished instantaneously. Should he wish for] a child, its conception, delivery, and growth will be accomplished in a moment, as he wishes." ...

134. All given extra power for sexual intercourse. *Mishkat*: Tirmidhi/Anas ibn Malik

The Prophet 🕊 said: "In the Garden the believers will be given such and such power to conduct sexual intercourse."

135. A huge tree with a phenomenal shadow. Muslim 40.6784: Abu Hurairah

The Messenger of Allah 🕊 has said: "In the Garden, there is a tree under the shadow of which a rider can travel for a hundred years."

136. Meeting place with large-eyed maidens. *Mishkat*: Tirmidhi/'Ali ibn Abi Talib

The Messenger of Allah 🕊 said: "In the Garden there is a meeting place for large-eyed maidens, who will raise voices such as created beings have never heard and say: 'We are the women who live forever, we are the women in affluent circumstances who will never be destitute, we are the women who are pleased and not displeased. Blessed are those who belong to us and to whom we belong!'"

137. A tent made of pearls, sixty miles high. Muslim 40.6806: Abu Bakr ibn Abu Musa

The Messenger 🕊 said that in the Garden there would be a tent made of [pearls], whose height would be sixty miles; in each corner of which there would be a family of believers, out of the sight of other people.

138. Great rivers of water, honey, milk, and wine. *Mishkat*: Tirmidhi/Hakim ibn Mu'awiyah

The Messenger of Allah 🕊 said: "In the Garden there are four great rivers: one of water, one of honey, one of milk, and one of wine... ."

139. All trees have trunks in gold. *Mishkat*: Tirmidhi/Abu Hurairah

The Messenger of Allah 🕊 said: "The trunk of every tree in the Garden is of gold."

B. Degrees of the Garden

There are one hundred degrees in the Garden. The highest is named al-Firdaws - Paradise. It is the one for which any Muslim should ask.

However, supplications should not be exaggerated.

140. The highest Garden is al-Firdaws, below His throne.
Bukhari 9.519: Abu Hurairah

The Prophet 🕮 said: "[Allah has made it incumbent upon Him] to admit to the Garden any who believes in Him and His Messenger, establishes the prayer, and fasts in Ramadan - whether he emigrates for Allah's cause or stays in his homeland." The companions said, "Messenger of Allah! Should we not inform the people of that?" He said, "[Note, however, that] there are one-hundred degrees in the Garden, which Allah has prepared for those who carry on jihad in His cause. The distance between every two degrees is like the distance between the sky and the earth. So if you ask Allah for anything, ask Him for al-Firdaws, for it is the last and the highest part of the Garden. At its top is the Throne of Allah, and from it gush forth the rivers of the Garden."

141. The levels are separated like the stars in space.
Muslim 40.6788: Sahl ibn Sa'd

The Messenger of Allah 🕮 has said: "The inhabitants of [the lower apartments of] the Garden will look at the upper apartments of the Garden as you see the stars in the sky."

142. Martyred young, Harithah is in al-Firdaws.
Bukhari 5.318: Anas

Harithah was martyred at the battle of Badr, and he was a young boy then. His mother came to the Prophet 🕮 and said, "Messenger of Allah! You know how dear Harithah is to me. If he is in the Garden, I shall remain patient and hope for a reward from Allah... ." The Prophet 🕮 said, "May Allah be merciful to you! ... There are many Gardens and your son is in the Garden of al-Firdaws."

143. On avoiding excess in supplication.
Abu Dawud 1.96: 'Abdullah ibn Mughaffal

'Abdullah heard his son praying to Allah: "O Allah, I ask You for a white palace on the right of the Garden when I enter it." He said: "Son, simply ask Allah for the Garden and seek refuge in Him from the Fire. I heard the Messenger of Allah ﷺ say: 'In this community there will be some people who will exceed the limits in purification and in supplication.'"

III. GLIMPSES OF THE FIRE

This section first gives an idea of the scope of the Fire - its depth is seventy years of free fall and its fire seventy times harsher than the fire of this world - and then describes the inmates of the Fire and their suffering.

144. The Fire's depth is seventy years of free fall.
Muslim 40.6813: Abu Hurairah
Once in the company of the Prophet ﷺ we heard a terrible sound. Thereupon he asked: "Do you know what that was?" We said: "Allah and His Messenger know best." He then explained: "That was [the sound made by] a stone thrown seventy years ago in the Fire and that has been constantly falling down to reach its base only now."

145. The Fire is seventy times more severe than worldly fire.
Muwatta 57.1: Abu Hurairah
The Messenger of Allah ﷺ said: "The fire [in this world] is a seventieth part of the fire of Hell." His companions said: "Messenger of Allah, this fire is certainly enough." He insisted: "That fire is sixty-nine times greater."

146. The tooth of an unbeliever in the Fire is like Uhud.
Muslim 40.6831: Abu Hurairah
The Prophet ﷺ said: "The [tooth of an unbeliever in the Fire] will be like the mountain of Uhud, and the thickness of his skin a journey of three nights."

147. The shoulders of an unbeliever in the Fire will be a ride of three days.
Muslim 40.6832: Abu Hurairah
The Messenger of Allah ﷺ observed: "The distance between the shoulders of the unbeliever in the Fire will be a journey of three days for a swift rider."

148. A heated stone pressed on the breast.
Bukhari 2.489: Al-Ahnaf ibn Qays
While we were at a gathering, a man with very rough hair, clothes, and appearance came and stood in front of us. He greeted us and said, "Inform those who hoard wealth, that a stone will be heated in the Fire and pressed against their nipples till it comes out from their shoulder blades and then pressed against their shoulders till it comes through their breasts..." After saying that, he retreated to sit by a pillar. I went to sit beside him, not recognising him, and said: "I think the people disliked what you said." He replied: "These people do not understand anything; [it is my friend that told me that]." I asked: "Who is your friend?" He said: "The Prophet ﷺ told me: 'Abu Dharr! Do you see the mountain of Uhud? ... I do not like to have gold equal to it unless I spend it all [in Allah's cause] except three dinars. These people do not know the right thing to do and they collect worldly wealth..."

149. Least suffering: shoes of fire boiling the brain.
Muslim 1.0415: Nu'man ibn Bashir
The Prophet ﷺ said: "Verily the least suffering for the inmates of the Fire would be for him who would have to wear shoes and laces of Fire. Yet, his brain will boil with these, as does a cooking vessel. He will think that no one is in a more grievous torment than him, while he actually is in the least torment."

150. A special mountain for torturing the Fire's inmates.
Mishkat: Tirmidhi/Abu Said
The Messenger of Allah ﷺ said, "There is a mountain in the Fire, which people will be made to climb for seventy years and [crawl down] a similar distance, and so on forever."

Chapter 7: Ways to the Garden or the Fire

This chapter is the most important of all, as it is the one addressing the prime objective of the book. Containing more than two fifths of the compilation, it is divided into three sections pertaining to the main duties prescribed in Islam, kindness and good dealings with people, and others deeds. Needless to say, the ways to the Garden and those to the Fire are contradictory; following the former implies avoiding the latter and vice versa. Besides, a comprehensive enumeration is impossible since every deed is taken into account and leads, to some extent, to either the Garden or the Fire. The hadith compiled here concern some of the deeds about which it is mentioned that they are either a direct way to the Garden or to the Fire. It should be remembered, once again, that this compilation is only a supplement to the Qur'an. The gateways to either the Garden or the Fire are all spelled out in the Glorious Book, and in the most authoritative style.

I. FULFILLING THE MAIN DUTIES OF ISLAM

A. IMAN

Faith (*iman*) is not a deed per se. But it is the motive for the first prescribed deed, the solemn testimony (*shahadah*) that there is no god except Allah and the Prophet Muhammad ﷺ is His messenger. Furthermore, iman is directly involved in all other deeds; in fact it is traditionally believed to be proportionally increasing with them. After defining iman, the hadith that follow provide clarifications on its significance and importance in the Judgement process, and finally show that even the most truthful companions of the Prophet ﷺ used to doubt their own iman - which contributed to their strengthening it.

151. What is Islam, what is iman, what is ihsan?

Muslim 1.0001: 'Umar ibn al-Khattab

While we were sitting with the Messenger of Allah ﷺ one day a man came up to us whose clothes were extremely white, whose hair was extremely black, upon whom traces of travelling could not be seen, and whom none of us knew, until he sat down close to the Prophet, may Allah bless with him and grant him peace, so that he rested his knees upon his knees and placed his two hands upon his thighs and said, "Muhammad, tell me about Islam." The Messenger of Allah ﷺ said, "Islam is that you witness that there is no god but Allah and that Muhammad is the Messenger of Allah, and you establish the prayer, and you give the Zakat, and you fast Ramadan, and you perform the Hajj of the House if you are able to take a way to it." He said, "You have told the truth," and we were amazed at him asking him and [then] telling him that he told the truth.

He said, "Tell me about Iman." He said, "That you affirm Allah, His angels, His books, His messengers, and the Last Day, and that you affirm the Decree, the good of it and the bad of it." He said, "You have told the truth."

He said, "Tell me about Ihsan." He said, "That you worship Allah as if you see Him, for if you don't see Him then truly He sees you."

He said, "Tell me about the Hour." He said, "The one asked about it knows no more than the one asking." He said, "Then tell me about its signs." He said, "That the female slave should give birth to her mistress, and you see poor, naked, barefoot shepherds of sheep and goats competing in raising buildings."

He went away, and I remained some time. Then he said, "Umar, do you know who the questioner was?" I said, "Allah and His Messenger know best." He said, "He was Jibril who came to you to teach you your deen".

152. Weeping, doing jihad out of faith.
Mishkat: Tirmidhi/Abu Hurairah

The Prophet ﷺ is reported to have said that "a person who sheds tears out of the fear of Allah will not go to the Fire till the milk returns into the breasts," which is impossible. He also observed that "the dust produced in jihad and the smoke of the Fire will never co-exist," that is, the person who is so God-fearing as to take part in jihad shall not experience the torment of the Fire.

153. Those who love one another, affirming iman, are for the Garden.
Muslim 1.0096: Abu Hurairah

The Prophet ﷺ observed: "You shall not enter the Garden so long as you do not affirm belief [in all the articles of faith], and you will not believe as long as you do not love one another. Should I not direct you to a thing that will foster love amongst you: Give currency to the practice of paying salutation to one another by saying 'As-salamu 'alaikum!'"

154. Faith implies treating others like oneself.
Bukhari 1.12: Anas

The Prophet ﷺ said, "None of you will have faith till he wishes for his [Muslim] brother what he wishes for himself."

155. Faithful Muslims behave well towards their wives.
Mishkat: Tirmidhi/Abu Hurairah

The Prophet ﷺ once said: "The perfect Muslim in terms of faith is one who has excellent behaviour; and the best among you are those who behave best toward their wives."

156. Handhalah and Abu Bakr doubt their own iman.
Muslim 37.6623: Handhalah Usayyidi

I once met Abu Bakr [and told him]: "Handhalah has turned out to be a hypocrite." He said: "Hallowed be Allah, what are you saying?" Thereupon I [Handhalah] said: "When we are in the company of the Prophet ﷺ we ponder over the Fire and the Garden as if we were seeing them with our very eyes. But when we are away from him we attend to our families and businesses, and most of these things [pertaining to the

Hereafter] slip out of our minds." Abu Bakr said: "By Allah, I also experience the same thing." Thus Abu Bakr and I went to the Messenger of Allah ﷺ and explained our problem. Thereupon the Prophet ﷺ said: "By Him in Whose hand is my life, if your state of mind remained the same as it is in my presence and you were always busy in remembrance [of Allah and the Hereafter], the angels would come down and shake hands with you in your beds and in your streets. But, Handhalah, time should be devoted [to the worldly affairs] and time [should be devoted to prayer and meditation]." He said this three times.

157. 'Abd ar-Rahman ibn 'Awf doubts his iman.
Bukhari 2.365: Ibrahim
Once a meal was brought to 'Abd ar-Rahman ibn 'Awf. ... He said, "Mus'ab ibn Umar was martyred and he was better than I. He was shrouded in his cloak and when his head was covered with it his legs became bare, and when his legs were covered his head became uncovered. Hamzah was martyred and he was better than I. Now worldly wealth has been bestowed upon us. No doubt, I fear that the rewards of my deeds might have been given in this world [and nothing remains for me in the Hereafter]." Then he started weeping and left his food.

B. SALAT

Salat is the first action to be reckoned in the Judgement process. It is the most effective tool for bringing one near to the Almighty as well as a suitable way of expressing one's gratitude to Him. Perfect salat from someone who has a pure tawhid without overt or covert ascription of partners to Allah, along with the fulfilment of the other obligations of Islam and avoidance of the prohibitions, may be considered a guarantee of the Garden, and abandoning salat is purely disbelief.

158. Salat at its proper time is the best deed.
Muslim 1.0152: 'Abdullah ibn Mas'ud
I once asked the Messenger of Allah ﷺ which of the deeds takes one nearer to the Garden. He replied: "Prayer at its proper time." I said: "What is next, Messenger of Allah?" He replied: "Kindness to parents." I said: "What next?" He replied: "Jihad in the cause of Allah."

159. Guarantee for regularly performed salat.
Abu Dawud 2.430: Abu Qatadah
The Prophet ﷺ once said: "Allah, exalted is He, said: 'I made five times salat obligatory on your people, and I took a guarantee that whoever observes them regularly at their times shall be admitted to the Garden; to those who do not offer them regularly, there is no such guarantee.'"

160. Rewards for specific salats.
Abu Dawud 2.427: 'Umarah ibn Ruwaybah
The Messenger of Allah ﷺ is reported to have said: "No one will enter the Fire who has performed salat before the rising of the sun and before its setting [probably meaning who has regularly performed the dawn and the afternoon salats and consequently the other salats in between]."

161. The first thing checked on the Day.
Abu Dawud 3.863: Abu Hurairah
The Prophet ﷺ is believed to have said: "The first thing about which the people will be called to account on the Day of Judgement is salat. Our Lord, exalted is He, will say to the angels, though He knows best, 'Look into the salat of My slave and see whether he has offered it perfectly or imperfectly.' If it is perfect, that will be recorded as perfect. If it is defective, He will say: 'See whether there are some optional salats offered by My slave.' If there are optional salats to his credit, He will say: 'Compensate the obligatory salats by the optional salats for My slave.' Then all the [other] actions will be assessed similarly."

162. The Prophet's gratitude to Allah expressed through salat.
Muslim 39.6772: Mughirah ibn Shu'bah
The Prophet ﷺ performed salat so much so that his feet were swollen. Thus, he was asked by one of his spouses: "Allah has pardoned your earlier and later wrong actions [why do you still undergo so much hardship]?" Thereupon he said: "May I not then prove myself to be a grateful slave?"

163. Special reward for Bilal's extra salats. *Mishkat*: Tirmidhi/ Buraydah ibn al-Hasib
One morning the Prophet ﷺ called Bilal and said: "What did you do

to get to the Garden before me? I have never entered the Garden without hearing the rustling of your garments in front of me." He replied, "Messenger of Allah, I have never made the call to salat without performing a two rak'ah salat, and no impurity has ever happened to me without my performing ablution on the spot and thinking that I owed Allah two rak'ahs."

164. Each prostration raises us a degree.
Muslim 4.0989: Ma'dan ibn Talhah
Thawban was asked about an act that makes a person admitted to the Garden. He said: "I asked the Messenger of Allah ﷺ about that and he said: 'Make frequent prostrations before Allah, for you will not make one prostration without raising yourself one degree because of it, and removing one wrong action from you, because of it.'"

165. Whoever gives up salat falls into disbelief.
Mishkat: Tirmidhi/Buraydah ibn al-Hasib
The Prophet ﷺ said: "What distinguishes us from the unbelievers and the hypocrites is our commitment to salat. Whoever gives up salat falls into disbelief."

C. SADAQAH

Sadaqah, i.e. optional acts of generosity, acts in a complex manner. A small amount of sadaqah, even half a date, can save someone from the Fire. Conversely, refusal to pay even the obligatory zakat is a real source of torment on the Day of Judgement itself, before the sentences are pronounced. It is important to distinguish between those acts of sadaqah and the pillar of zakat itself which is collected by an amir on cattle, crops and people's cash and the proceeds of their businesses, and then distributed to the poor, the needy, and the other categories mentioned in the Qur'an.

166. Even half a date can save one from the Fire.
Muslim 5.2215: 'Adi ibn Hatim
The Messenger of Allah ﷺ has said: "He who among you can protect himself against the Fire should do so, even if it should be with half a date."

167. What the Prophet ﷺ would do with his gold.
Bukhari 9.334: Abu Hurairah
The Prophet, peace be upon him said, "If I had gold equal to the mountain of Uhud, I would love that, before three days had passed, not a single dinar thereof remained with me, if I found somebody to accept it, excluding some amount that I would keep for the payment of my debts."

168. Better to be generous than pious but stingy.
Mishkat: Tirmidhi/Abu Hurairah
The Messenger of Allah ﷺ said: "The generous man is near to Allah, near to the Garden, near to men and far from the Fire, but the miserly man is far from Allah, far from the Garden, far from [the good] men and near to the Fire. Indeed, an ignorant man who is generous is dearer to Allah than a [learned] worshipper who is miserly."

D. FASTING

The gates of the Garden are open during the entire month of Ramadan. Fasting itself has a special gate into the Garden: ar-Rayyan. Most importantly, the reward for fasting is paid directly by Allah.

169. The gates of the Garden are opened in Ramadan.
Bukhari 4.497: Abu Hurairah
The Messenger of Allah ﷺ said: "When the month of Ramadan comes, the gates of the Garden are opened, the gates of the Fire closed, and the devils chained."

170. The reward for fasting is directly paid by Allah.
Bukhari 3.128: Abu Hurairah
The Messenger of Allah ﷺ said: "Allah said, 'All the deeds of Adam's sons are for them, except fasting, which is for Me, and I will give the reward for it.' Fasting is a shield or protection from the Fire and from committing wrong actions. If one of you is fasting, he should avoid sexual intercourse and quarrelling - and if somebody should fight or quarrel with him, he should say, 'I am fasting.' By Him in Whose hand my self is, the unpleasant smell coming from the mouth of a fasting person is better with Allah than the smell of musk. There are two pleas-

ures for the fasting persons, one at the time of breaking the fast, and the other at the time of meeting Allah [when they reap the special reward readied for the fasting slaves]."

171. Ar-Rayyan, the gate to the Garden for those who fast.
Bukhari 3.120: Sahl
The Prophet ﷺ said: "There is a gate in the Garden called ar-Rayyan, and only those who observe fast will enter through it on the Day of Rising. It will be said, 'Where are those who used to observe fasts?' They will get up [and enter.] After their entry the gate will be closed."

E. Hajj
Performing hajj purifies the hajji as though he or she were born anew. Dying in hajj is compared to dying in jihad.

172. The hajji is purified as if born anew.
Bukhari 2.596: Abu Hurairah
The Prophet ﷺ said: "Whoever performs hajj for Allah's pleasure and neither sleeps with his wife nor commits evil deeds will return [home free from all wrong actions] as if he were born anew."

173. Reward for an 'umrah is expiation of wrong actions, but for hajj it is the Garden.
Bukhari 3.1: Abu Hurairah
The Messenger of Allah ﷺ said: "The performance of 'umrah is an expiation for the wrong actions committed [between it and the previous one], and the reward for a hajj [accepted by Allah] is nothing but the Garden."

174. Those who die on hajj are like shuhada'.
Muslim 7.2752: Sa'id ibn Jubayr
A camel broke the neck of its owner while he was in the state of ihram and he was at that time in the company of the Prophet ﷺ. The latter commanded that the deceased should be bathed with water mixed with leaves of the lotus tree, that no perfume should be applied to him, and that his head should be uncovered, for he would be raised on the Day of Rising pronouncing *talbiyah* [the invocation made during hajj].

II. KINDNESS AND GOOD DEALINGS WITH OTHER BEINGS

Kindness and sound dealings with people are highly valued in Islam. This is all the more understandable as Muslims are required to live in society, and social life is impossible without mutual good behaviour. This section is broadly divided into five subsections respectively listing hadith on (1) general conduct, (2) attitude toward relatives and neighbours, (3) public office, (4) respect of other people's property and rights, and (5) kindness to animals.

A. GENERAL CONDUCT

One should watch one's general conduct, not only avoiding harming other people but also aiming to serve them, directly and indirectly. Breathtakingly, the hadith explain that maintaining sound relationships inside the Muslim community is "better than fasting, praying, and sadaqah."

175. Nothing is weightier than good behaviour. *Mishkat*: Tirmidhi/Abu al-Darda

The Prophet ﷺ said that nothing is weightier in the scales of a believer on the Day of Judgement than his good behaviour; Allah treats with displeasure a person who is given to loose and vulgar talk.

176. The Fire for an uncontrolled mouth or private parts. *Mishkat*: Tirmidhi/Abu Hurairah

The Prophet ﷺ once said: "Do you know the thing that most commonly brings people into the Garden? It is fear of Allah and good character. Do you know what most commonly brings people into the Fire? It is the two hollow things: the mouth and the private parts [this can be understood as harming the Muslims through lying, cursing, and similar acts of the mouth, or through adultery]."

177. The Garden won by removing trash and harmful things from the road. Muslim 32.6340: Abu Hurairah

The Prophet ﷺ said: "A person, seeing tree branches on the road said, 'By Allah, I shall remove these branches from here so that they may not harm the Muslims.' Through that act he won admission to the Garden."

178. Cutting the lotus tree leads to the Fire.
Abu Dawud 41.5220: 'Abdullah ibn Habashi

The Prophet ﷺ said: "Whoever cuts the lotus tree [which was used for several purposes, including hygiene and purification, by both men and women], will be brought by Allah headlong into the Fire."

179. Controlling anger with slaves, thus avoiding the Fire.
Muslim 15.4088: Abu Mas'ud al-Ansari

I was once beating a slave of mine and suddenly heard a voice behind me, saying: "Abu Mas'ud, bear in mind that Allah has more dominance over you than you have over him." I turned back and found the speaker to be the Prophet ﷺ. I said: "the Messenger of Allah, I set him free for the sake of Allah." Thereupon he said: "Had you not done that, the Fire would have opened [its gates for you.]"

180. Treating people like oneself leads to the Garden.
Muslim 20.4546: 'Abdullah ibn 'Amr

While in a gathering, the Prophet ﷺ said: "It was the duty of every prophet before me to guide his followers to what he knew was good for them and warn them against what he knew was bad for them. Whoever wishes to be delivered from the Fire and enter the Garden should die with iman in Allah and the Last Day and should treat people as he wishes to be treated by them."

181. The Garden delayed until reconciliation.
Muslim 32.6222: Abu Hurairah

The Prophet ﷺ said: "The gates of the Garden are only opened on two days, Monday and Thursday, and then every slave of Allah who does not associate anything with Allah is granted pardon, except the person in whose [heart] there is rancour against his brother: It will be said [three times]: 'Look towards both of them until there is reconciliation.'"

182. "I was sick but you did not visit Me."
Muslim 32.6232: Abu Hurairah

The following dialogue, according to the Prophet ﷺ will take place on the Day of Rising: "Son of Adam," the Almighty will say, "I was sick but you did not visit Me." His interlocutor will say: "My Lord, how could I visit You when You are the Lord of the worlds?" Thereupon He will say: "Did not you know that such and such a slave of Mine was sick but failed to visit him? Were you not aware that if you had visited him, you would have found Me by him?"

"Son of Adam, I asked you for food but you did not feed Me." He will say: "My Lord, how could I feed you when you are the Lord of the worlds?" The Almighty will say: "Did not such and such a slave of Mine ask food from you but you failed to feed him, and were you not aware that if you had fed him you would have found him beside Me?"

"Son of Adam, I asked for drink but you did not provide Me." He will reply: "My Lord, how could I provide it to the Lord of the worlds?" Thereupon the Almighty will say: "Such and such a slave of Mine asked you for a drink but you did not provide him, and had you provided him the drink you would have found him near to Me."

183. Forgiveness for leniency shown to straitened people.
Muslim 10.3792: Abu Mas'ud

The Prophet ﷺ once said: "A [rich man] from the people who lived before you was called to account and no good was found [except that he had good dealings] with people and had commanded his servants to show leniency to the straitened ones. Upon this, Allah [overlooked his faults]."

184. What is better than fasting, praying ...
Abu Dawud 41.4901: Abu al-Darda

The Prophet ﷺ said: "Shall I not inform you of something better than fasting, praying, and sadaqah?" The people replied: "Yes, Prophet of Allah!" He said: "It is putting things right between people."

185. The Fire for abandoning a brother more than three days.
Abu Dawud 41.4896: Abu Hurairah

The Prophet ﷺ said: "It is not allowed for a Muslim to keep apart from his brother more than three days, because one who dies while doing so shall enter the Fire."

186. The Garden for visiting a brother.
Mishkat: Tirmidhi/Abu Hurairah

The Prophet ﷺ said that when a Muslim visits his brother, the Almighty will say, "You are happy and your walking is happy; you will come to an abode in the Garden."

B. ATTITUDE TOWARD RELATIVES AND NEIGHBOURS

The people close to a person, by either kinship or neighbourhood, are the first who are entitled to his or her good treatment. Severing one's family ties, just like harming one's neighbours, is implanting a huge barrier in one's way to the Garden.

187. Severing ties of kinship leads to the Fire.
Muslim 32.6199: Jubayr ibn Mut'im
The Prophet ﷺ said: "The one who severs ties of kinship will not enter the Garden."

188. Gaining the Garden because of aging parents.
Muslim 32.6189: Abu Hurairah
The Messenger of Allah ﷺ once said: "Let him be humiliated into dust! Let him be humiliated into dust!" It was said: "Messenger of Allah, who is he?" He said: "He who sees either one or both of his parents in their old age but does not enter the Garden." [The probable meaning is someone who is with his or her parents in their old age but does not take care of them, thus missing the reward for that great action - the Garden.]

189. Parents are their children's Heaven or Hell. *Mishkat*: Ibn Majah/Abu Umamah
A man asked the Prophet ﷺ : "Messenger of Allah, what rights do parents have over their children?" He replied, "They are your Garden and your Fire."

190. The Garden for giving daughters one's food.
Muslim 32.6363: A'ishah
A poor woman came to me along with her two daughters. I gave her three dates. She gave one date to each of the girls and then brought the remaining date to her mouth. But the girls expressed the desire to eat that one too, so she divided it between them. That act impressed me and I mentioned it to the Prophet ﷺ . Thereupon he said: "Verily Allah has assured the Garden for her because of that act."

191. Women pleasing their husbands for the Garden.
Mishkat: Ibn Majah/Umm Salamah

The Prophet ﷺ said: "If a woman dies while her husband is pleased with her, she will enter the Garden."

192. The Garden is at our mothers' feet. *Mishkat*: Ahmad/ Mu'awiyah ibn Jahimah

Jahimah came to the Prophet ﷺ and said: "Messenger of Allah, I desire to go on a military expedition and I have come to consult you." The Prophet ﷺ asked him whether his mother was alive, and when he replied affirmatively, he said: "Stay with her, for [your] Garden is at her feet."

193. Harming neighbours is an obstacle to the Garden.
Muslim 1.0074: Abu Hurairah

The Prophet ﷺ once said: "He will not enter the Garden whose neighbour is not secure from his wrongful conduct."

[A similar hadith, Bukhari 8.45, quotes the Prophet ﷺ as saying, "By Allah, he does not believe … that person whose neighbour does not feel safe from his evil."]

194. What are the greatest wrong actions?
Bukhari 6.4: Abdullah

I asked the Prophet ﷺ, "What is the greatest wrong action in the sight of Allah?" He said, "That you set up a rival to Allah, though He Alone created you." I said, "That is indeed a great wrong action," and asked: "What is next?" He said, "To kill your child lest he should share your food." I asked again, "What is next?" He said, "To commit adultery with the wife of your neighbour."

195. Neighbours are almost heirs.
Bukhari 8.43: A'ishah

The Prophet ﷺ said: "Jibril continued to recommend me to treat neighbours kindly and politely to such an extent that I thought he would order me to take them as my heirs."

C. PUBLIC OFFICE

Public office can generate special rewards but it involves extra duties.

The official is a trustee: As well as exemplifying right personal behaviour, he or she is supposed to see to it that justice and law and order are maintained properly and fairly vis-à-vis all members of society.

196. A special sign for those guilty of a breach of trust.
Muslim 19.4310: Abu Sa'id

The Messenger of Allah ﷺ said: "On the Day of Judgement there will be a flag for every person guilty of a breach of trust. It will be raised in proportion to the guilt, and there is no guilt of treachery more serious than the one committed by a ruler."

197. Just leaders are near to Him, tyrants are far away.
Mishkat: Tirmidhi/Abu Sa'id

The Prophet ﷺ said: "The one who will be dearest to Allah and nearest to Him in station on the Day of Rising will be a just leader, and the one who will be most hateful to Allah on the Day of Rising and will receive the severest punishment will be a tyrannical leader."

198. Concealing even a needle can lead to trouble.
Muslim 20.4514: 'Adi ibn Amira al-Kindi

I heard the Prophet ﷺ say: "Whoever of you is appointed by us to a position of authority and conceals from us a needle or something smaller than that will have committed misappropriation of public funds and will have to produce it on the Day of Judgement."

199. The Muslim's honour is sacred.
Abu Dawud 41.4863: Al-Mustawrid

The Prophet ﷺ said: "If anyone eats once at the cost of a Muslim's honour, Allah will feed him with a similar amount of the Fire; if anyone clothes himself with a garment at the cost of a Muslim's honour, Allah will clothe him with a similar amount of the Fire; and if anyone puts himself in a position of reputation and showing off [ostentation] Allah will disgrace him with a place of reputation and showing off on the Day of Rising."

200. Authority is a trust, and is not for the weak.
Muslim 20.4491: Abu Dharr

I once made the following request to the Prophet ﷺ : "Messenger of

Allah, will you not appoint me to a public office?" He stroked my shoulder with his hand and said: "Abu Dharr, you are weak, and authority is a trust: On the Day of Judgement it is a cause of humiliation and repentance, except for those who fulfil its obligations."

201. Judges are of three kinds, but only one goes to the Garden. Abu Dawud 24.3566: Buraydah ibn al-Hasib

The Prophet ﷺ said: "Judges are of three types, one of whom will go to the Garden and the other two to the Fire. The judges who will go to the Garden are those who know what is right and give judgements accordingly; the judges who will go to the Fire are those who know what is right but act tyrannically in their judgements and those who give judgements ignorantly."

202. Opposing Allah's laws leads to the Fire. Abu Dawud 24.3590: 'Abdullah ibn 'Umar

The Messenger of Allah ﷺ said: "If someone's intercession intervenes as an obstacle to one of the punishments prescribed by Allah, he has opposed Allah; if anyone disputes knowingly about something that is false, he remains in the displeasure of Allah till he desists; and if anyone makes an untruthful accusation against a Muslim, he will be made to dwell in the corrupt fluid flowing from the inhabitants of the Fire till he retracts his statement."

203. Better forgive a guilty person than punish an innocent person. *Mishkat*: Tirmidhi/A'ishah

The Messenger of Allah ﷺ said, "As much as possible [without undermining the hadd punishments], avert the prescribed penalties from Muslims, and if there is any way out then let a man go; for it is better for a leader to make a mistake in forgiving than to make a mistake in punishing."

D. ATTITUDE TOWARD PEOPLE'S PROPERTY AND RIGHTS

Misappropriation in any form - stealing, taking illegal taxes, taking more zakat than necessary, failing to pay debts, begging while not in need, and so forth - is extremely dangerous. It may lead the guilty directly to the Fire or sway the effects of their most valued actions, such as jihad. As regards people's rights, acts like looking at someone's letter without permission that may appear only to be minor wrong actions, can in reality be tickets to the Fire.

204. Begging while not in need is begging for the Fire.
Abu Dawud 9.1625: Sahl ibn Hanzaliyyah

The Prophet ﷺ said: "He who begs when he has sufficiency is simply asking for a large amount of the Fire."

205. Better to sell firewood than to beg.
Bukhari 2.550: az-Zubayr ibn al-'Awwam

The Prophet ﷺ said, "Any of you would do better to take a rope and fetch a bundle of firewood on his back and sell it [to get money] - thus Allah will save his face from the Fire - rather than ask from people, who may give him or not."

206. Missing the Garden because of excessive taxation.
Abu Dawud 19.2931: 'Uqbah ibn 'Amir

I heard the Messenger of Allah ﷺ say: "One who wrongfully takes an extra tax [over and above zakat, or possibly taking too much zakat] will not enter the Garden."

207. Dying as a shaheed clears all lapses except debts.
Muslim 20.4646: Abu Qatadah

The Prophet ﷺ stood up among his companions to deliver a khutbah, in which he told them that jihad in the way of Allah and iman in Allah are the most meritorious acts. A man stood up and said: "Messenger of Allah, do you think that if I am killed in the way of Allah, my wrong actions will be blotted out for me?" The Prophet ﷺ said: "Yes, if you are killed in the way of Allah, while you are patient and sincere, always fighting the enemy, never turning away." The man asked for more confirmation: "Do you really think if I am killed in the way of Allah, all my wrong actions will be obliterated for me?" The Prophet ﷺ said: "[Yes indeed! All your lapses will be forgiven], except debt: Jibril has [just] told me that."

208. The soul is attached to a debt until it is paid.
Mishkat: Shafi'i/Abu Hurairah

The Prophet ﷺ on one occasion said: "A believer's soul is attached to his debt till it is paid."

209. Stealing a garment nullifies reward for jihad.
Muslim 1.0209: Umar ibn al-Khattab

On the day of the battle of Khaybar, some companions of the Prophet ﷺ, talking of the dead Muslims, mentioned one person thus: "So and so is a shaheed." But the Prophet ﷺ remarked: "Nay, not so verily: I have seen him in the Fire for the garment that he had stolen from the booty."

210. Freedom from debt, freedom from Fire. *Mishkat*: Tirmidhi/Thawban

The Messenger of Allah ﷺ said: "Anyone who dies free from pride, faithlessness regarding the spoils, and debt, will enter the Garden."

211. Allah is against three persons on the Day.
Bukhari 3.430: Abu Hurairah

The Prophet ﷺ said: "Allah says, 'I will be against three persons on the Day of Rising: (1) one who makes a covenant in My Name but proves treacherous, (2) one who sells a free person and uses the price, and (3) one who employs a labourer and gets the full work done but does not pay the labourer."

212. Wrongly depriving heirs leads to the Fire. *Mishkat*: Ibn Majah/Anas ibn Malik

The Prophet ﷺ said, "If anyone deprives an heir of his inheritance, Allah will deprive him of his inheritance in the Garden."

213. Rewards lost to others in return for harm.
Muslim 32.6251: Abu Hurairah

The Prophet ﷺ said: "Do you know who is poor?" His companions said: "A poor person amongst us is someone who has neither dirham nor wealth." He said: "The poor person of my community is he who will come on the Day of Rising with salats, fasts, and zakat but become bankrupt for having hurled abuse at others, slandered others, unlawfully consumed the wealth of others, shed the blood of others, and beat others: His virtues will be credited to the account of [his victims], and if his good deeds fall short of clearing his wrong actions, he will be thrown into the Fire."

214. Taking others' rights is taking the Fire.
Bukhari 3.638: Umm Salamah
Hearing some people quarrelling at his door, the Prophet 艐 came out, saying, "I am only a human, and opponents come to me [to settle their disputes]. One of you might present his case more eloquently than the other, whereby I may consider him right and give a verdict in his favour. So, if I give the right of a Muslim to another by mistake, then it is really a portion of Fire: He has the option to take it or give it up."

215. Looking at someone's letter may be looking at the Fire.
Abu Dawud 8.1480: 'Abdullah ibn 'Abbas
The Prophet 艐 once said: "He who looks at the letter of his brother without his permission looks at the Fire."

E. KINDNESS TO ANIMALS

Kindness should not be limited to human beings; it should encompass all other creatures around us. Imprisoning a cat until it died sent a person to the Fire, while quenching the thirst of a dog sent another person to the Garden.

216. A women was put in the Fire for starving a cat to death.
Muslim 37.6638: Abu Hurairah
The Prophet 艐 is reported as saying that a woman was thrown into the Fire because of a cat that she had tied and refused to feed until it slowly died from starvation.

217. The Garden for giving water to a dog.
Bukhari 1.174: Abu Hurairah
The Prophet 艐 said: "A man seeing a dog eating mud because of the severity of its thirst took a shoe, filled it with water, and kept on pouring water for the dog till it quenched its thirst. Thus Allah approved of his deed and made him to enter the Garden."

218. Cursed for using live creatures as targets.
Muslim 21.4816: Sa'id ibn Jubayr
Ibn 'Umar happened to pass by some young men of the Quraysh who had tied a bird at which they had been shooting arrows. No sooner did

they see Ibn 'Umar than they went away. Thereupon Ibn 'Umar said: "Who has done this? The Messenger of Allah 鬃 invoked a curse upon a marksman who uses a live thing as a target."

III. SPECIFIC DEEDS

A. JIHAD: A SECURE WAY TO HEAVEN

The importance of jihad is easily understandable, considering the role it played in affirming Islam in its early days. Nowadays, the chances of taking part in genuine jihad are fewer - which is all to the good, as peaceful Islam does not advocate war - but whenever a chance comes to fight for the sake of Allah, one should make the best of it and secure the Garden. As a matter of fact, shuhada' automatically enter the Garden, where their enjoyment is so great that they will want to come back to this life and be killed again and again, for the sake of Allah. More than simply saving themselves from the Fire, jihad victims will have the possibility of interceding for others. In fact, without dying in action, simple participation in the fight results in general forgiveness from Allah. Nevertheless, the reward for being a shaheed does not encompass the hypocrites, nor does it obliterate other people's rights (like debts, as seen earlier).

219. Hypocrites dying in jihad do not go to the Garden.
Mishkat: Darimi/'Utbah
The Prophet 鬃 said: "War victims are of three types: [1] a real believer who strives with his property and his person in Allah's cause and when he meets the enemies fights them till he is killed; [2] a believer who mingles a good deed with an evil one, who fights with his person and his property in Allah's cause till he is killed when he meets the enemies; and [3] a hypocrite who strives with his person and his property, and when he meets the enemies fights till he is killed. [The first two will enter the Garden, but the last one] will go to the Fire, because the sword does not obliterate hypocrisy."

220. Shuhada' wish to come back and be killed again.
Muslim 20.4635: Anas ibn Malik

The Prophet ﷺ once said: "Nobody who enters the Garden would ever like to return to this world - even if he were offered everything on the surface of the earth as an inducement - except the shaheed. The shaheed will desire to return to this world and be killed ten times for the great honour that has been bestowed upon him."

221. Both the killer and the victim go to the Garden.
Muslim 20.4658: Abu Hurairah

The Messenger of Allah ﷺ said: "Allah laughs at two men, both of whom will enter the Garden though one of them unlawfully kills the other." His companions said: "Messenger of Allah, how is it possible?" He said: "One of them fights in the way of Allah and dies a shaheed. Then Allah turns in mercy to the murderer too, makes him embrace Islam, fight in His way and die a shaheed."

222. Discarding dates, fighting to become a shaheed.
Muslim 20.4678: Jabir

During a battle, a man asked: "Messenger of Allah, where shall I be if I am killed?" He ﷺ replied: "In the Garden." The man threw away what he had in his hand - dates which he was eating - and fought until he was killed."

223. Shuhada' receive six good things from Allah. *Mishkat*: Tirmidhi/Al-Miqdam

The Messenger of Allah ﷺ said: "The shaheed receives six good things from Allah: [1] He is forgiven at the first shedding of his blood; [2] he is shown his abode in the Garden; [3] he is preserved from the punishment in the grave; [4] he is kept safe from the greatest terror; [5] he has placed on his head the crown of honour, a ruby of which is better than the world and what it contains; [6] he is married to seventy-two wives of the maidens with large dark eyes and is made intercessor for seventy of his relatives."

224. Maybe the veterans of Badr can "do whatever they like."
Bukhari 5.319: Ali

The Messenger of Allah ﷺ sent Abu Marthad, az-Zubayr, and I on horses with this instruction: "Go till you reach Rawdat-Khakh, there is a pagan woman carrying a letter from Hatib ibn Abi Balta'ah to the pagans of Makkah."

We went and found the women riding a camel at the place indicated by the Prophet of Allah and asked her to give us the letter. She said, "I have no letter." Then we made her camel kneel down and searched her, but we found no letter. Then we said, "Certainly the Messenger of Allah had told us the truth. Take out the letter, otherwise we shall strip you!" When she saw that we were determined, she put her hand below her belt - for she had tied her cloak round her waist - and took out the letter.

When we brought her to the Messenger of Allah, 'Umar said: "Messenger of Allah, Hatib has betrayed Allah, His Messenger, and the believers! Let me cut his neck!" The Prophet ﷺ asked Hatib, "What made you do this?" Hatib said, "By Allah, I did not intend to give up my belief in Allah and His Messenger, but I wanted to have some influence among the [Makkan] people so that Allah might protect my family and property. There is none of your companions but has some of his relatives there, through whom Allah protects his family and property."

The Prophet ﷺ said, "He has told the truth; do not say anything to him but good." 'Umar said, "He has betrayed Allah, His Messenger, and the faithful believers. Let me cut off his head!" The Prophet ﷺ said, "Is he not one of the soldiers of Badr? Maybe Allah looked at the Badr warriors and said, 'Do whatever you like, as I have granted the Garden to you' or 'I have forgiven you.'" On this, tears came out of 'Umar's eyes, and he said: "Allah and His Messenger know better."

B. ARROGANCE AND PRIDE: EXPRESSWAYS TO THE FIRE

Glory and pride are for Allah. Some aspects of pride, therefore, pertain to shirk: associating oneself with Allah. Pride is also associated with disbelief, as it is partly defined as the denial of the truth. Nevertheless, the definition of pride and arrogance needs further clarification: Wearing neat clothes is not arrogance per se; whereas wearing them to show off and look down upon others is. Whoever has an iota of pride and arrogance in his or her heart needs to get rid of it in time, for these are expressways to the Fire.

225. Pride is the Almighty's cloak.
Abu Dawud 32.4079: Abu Hurairah
The Prophet 鬱 said: "Allah Most High says, 'Pride is My cloak, and majesty is My lower garment: I shall throw into the Fire any who competes with Me for them.'"

226. Proud people are resurrected in ignominy.
Mishkat: Tirmidhi/Abdullah ibn Amr
The Messenger of Allah 鬱 said: "On the Day of Rising, the proud will be resurrected like specks in the form of men, covered all around with ignominy. They will be driven to a prison in the Fire called Bawlas with the hottest fire rising over them, and they will be given to drink the liquid of the inhabitants of the Fire, which is *tinat al-khabal*."

227. The first men to be sentenced to the Fire.
Muslim 20.4688: Abu Hurairah
The Messenger of Allah 鬱 was heard saying which follows: "The first man whose case will be decided on the Day of Judgement will be a man who died a shaheed. As he is brought forth for Judgement, Allah will make him recount the blessings He bestowed upon him in this world and he will [admit having enjoyed them in his life]. Then the Almighty will say: 'What did you do [to repay these blessings]?' He will say: 'I fought for you until I died a shaheed.' Allah will say: 'You have told a lie. You fought so that you might be called a "brave warrior," and you were called so.' Then orders will be passed that he should be dragged with his face downward and cast into the Fire.

"Then a man will be brought forward who acquired knowledge and imparted it to others. Allah will make him recount His blessings, then ask: 'What did you do?' He will say: 'I acquired knowledge and disseminated it and recited the Qur'an, seeking your pleasure.' Allah will say: 'You have told a lie. You acquired knowledge so that you might be called "a scholar," and you recited the Qur'an so that it might be said: "He is a reciter," and such has been said.' Then orders will be passed that he should be dragged with his face downward and cast into the Fire.

"Then a man will be brought forward whom Allah had made abundantly rich and had granted every kind of wealth. Allah will make him recount His blessings, and ask him: 'What have you done?' He will say: 'I spent money in every cause in which you wished it to be spent.' Allah will say: 'You are lying. You did so only that it might be said about you: "He is a generous fellow," and so it was said.' Then orders will be passed that he should be dragged with his face downward and cast into the Fire."

228. The smallest amount of pride leads to the Fire.
Muslim 1.0164: 'Abdullah ibn Mas'ud
The Prophet ﷺ once observed: "He who has in his heart the weight of a mustard seed of pride will not enter the Garden." A person asked whether a person who "loves that his dress should be fine, and his shoes should be fine" would be taken to be acting in pride or arrogance. The Prophet ﷺ explained: "Allah is Graceful and He loves grace. Pride is disdaining the truth and looking down upon others."

229. Dragging clothes proudly, leads toward the Fire.
Bukhari 7.683: 'Abdullah ibn 'Umar
The Messenger of Allah ﷺ said that on the Day of Rising, Allah would not look at anyone who had dragged his clothes on the ground out of pride and arrogance.

C. Seeking and Disseminating Knowledge: Keys to the Garden

Seeking knowledge is similar to jihad. Once gained, knowledge should be disseminated as widely as possible, to benefit the entire community. A warning is necessary, however: Seeking and disseminating knowledge should be undertaken with genuine reasons, lest they should become keys to the Fire.

230. The road to knowledge is the road to the Garden.
Abu Dawud 25.3634: Abu'd-Darda

The Messenger of Allah ﷺ once said: "If anyone travels in search of knowledge, Allah will cause him to travel on one of the roads to the Garden. The angels will lower their wings in great pleasure with one who seeks knowledge, the inhabitants of the heavens and the earth and the fish in the deep waters will ask forgiveness for the learned man. The superiority of the learned man over the [ignorant] devout is like that of the moon, on the night when it is full, over the stars. The learned are the heirs of the Prophets, and the Prophets leave [only knowledge, not money] and he who takes it takes an abundant portion."

231. Path to knowledge, easy path to the Garden.
Muslim 34.6518: Abu Hurairah

The Messenger of Allah ﷺ once said: "Whoever removes an anxiety of the world from a believer, Allah will remove an anxiety of the Day of Resurrection from him. Whoever makes it easy for someone in difficulty, Allah will make it easy for him in the world and the Next Life. Whoever conceals [the wrong action of] a Muslim, Allah will conceal his [wrong action] in the world and the Next Life. Whoever travels on a path seeking in it knowledge, Allah will smooth for him a path by it to the Garden. A people do not gather in one of the houses of Allah, reciting the Book of Allah, studying it together and teaching it to each other, but that tranquility descends upon them, mercy covers them, the angels encircle them, and Allah remembers them among those who are with Him...."

232. Seekers of knowledge will be near the prophets.
Mishkat: Darimi/Al-Hasan al-Basri

The Prophet ﷺ said: "If a person dies while engaged in acquiring knowledge with a view to revive Islam with his knowledge, there will be [only] one degree between him and the prophets in the Garden."

233. Particular treatment for scholars. *Mishkat*: Baihaqi/Anas ibn Malik

The Prophet ﷺ once said: "The most generous among the people after me will be someone who acquires knowledge and then disseminates it.

On the Day of Rising he will receive a special treatment [like a king]."

234. Seeking knowledge for polemical purposes leads to the
Fire. *Mishkat*: Tirmidhi/Ka'b ibn Malik
The Messenger of Allah ﷺ said: "He who acquires knowledge in order
to fall into polemics with other scholars and prove his superiority over
them, or to dispute with the ignorant, or to attract the attention of
people, will be thrown into the Fire."

D. Lying, Backbiting, Slandering, and the Like are Slippery Roads Around the Fire

Islam being the "Religion of Truth," it is only understandable that truthfulness be a highly valued quality in Islam. Telling an untruth is par-
ticularly detrimental because of the evil consequences of dissension it
causes inside a society. Nevertheless, sometimes the truth should be
kept secret, and there are specific cases where not telling the truth is
forgivable.

235. Falsehood in general leads to the Fire.
Bukhari 8.116: Abdullah
The Prophet ﷺ said, "Truthfulness leads to taqwa, and taqwa leads to
the Garden: A man keeps on telling the truth until he becomes a truth-
ful person. Falsehood leads to wickedness, and wickedness leads to the
Fire: A man may keep on telling lies till he is written a liar before
Allah."

236. Makers of dissension accompany shaytan.
Muslim 39.6756: Jabir
The Prophet ﷺ once said: "Shaytan sends detachments of his own to
put people to trial, and the highest in rank in his eyes [and who thus is
to accompany him] is one who is most notorious in sowing the seed of
dissension."

237. What is backbiting?
Muslim 32.6265: Abu Hurairah
The Messenger of Allah ﷺ once asked: "Do you know what is backbit-
ing?" The Companions said: "Allah and His Messenger know best."

Thereupon he said: "Backbiting implies your talking about your brother in a manner that he does not like." It was then said to him: "What if I actually find in my brother what I mentioned?" He said: "[If what you mention is true,] you have actually backbitten him, and if [it is not true, you have committed] a slander."

238. The one punished in the grave for calumnies.
Bukhari 2.443: Ibn Abbas

The Prophet ﷺ once passed by two graves and explained that the persons inside were being tortured. He said, "They are being tortured not for great things [to avoid]. One of them never saved himself from soiling himself with his urine; the other went about with calumnies [making enmity between friends]." The Prophet ﷺ then took a green leaf of a palm tree, split it into two pieces, and fixed one on each grave. The people said, "Messenger of Allah! Why have you done so?" He replied: "I hope that their punishment may be lessened till [the leaf] become dry."

239. The Fire for interpreting Qur'an from opinion alone.
Mishkat: Tirmidhi/'Abdullah ibn 'Abbas

The Messenger of Allah ﷺ said: "Whoever speaks about the Qur'an on the basis of his personal opinion [alone] will find his abode in the Fire."

240. Discussing the divine decree is not recommended.
Mishkat: Ibn Majah/A'ishah

I heard the Messenger of Allah ﷺ saying: "Whoever discusses the Divine Decree [will be answerable for it on the Day of Rising.]"

241. Lying against the Prophet leads to the Fire.
Bukhari 1.106: 'Ali

The Prophet ﷺ said, "Do not tell a lie against me, for whoever does so shall surely enter the Fire."

242. All wrong actions forgiven except those made public.
Bukhari 8.95: Abu Hurairah

The Prophet ﷺ said: "All the wrong actions of my followers will be forgiven except those people who commit wrong actions openly or disclose them to the people. An example of such disclosure is that a person commits a wrong action at night, and, though Allah screens it from the public, he comes in the morning and says, 'So and so, I did this and that [evil] deed yesterday,' thus removing Allah's screen from himself."

243. White lies are permitted in three cases.
Mishkat: Ahmad/Asma bint Yazid

The Messenger of Allah ﷺ said, "Lying is allowable only in three cases: [1] falsehood spoken by a man to his wife to please her, [2] falsehood in war [that is, not telling the enemy the truth about the strategy of one's army], and [3] falsehood to put things right between people."

E. MISCELLANEOUS WAYS TO THE GARDEN OR THE FIRE

After mentioning a few more actions leading to the Fire, this last subsection lists a vast array of good deeds, emphasising their combination. Some of the combined items have appeared earlier on different occasions. Of the new negative items, making pictures is the most noticeable; among the positive items the prominent one is patience.

244. The Garden forbidden to the alcoholic, adulterer and liar.
Mishkat: Ahmad/'Abdullah ibn 'Umar

The Prophet ﷺ said: "There are three people to whom Allah has forbidden the Garden: [1] one who is addicted to wine, [2] an undutiful child, and [3] a cuckold who agrees to his womenfolk's adultery."

245. Ill-dressed women and tyrants in the Fire.
Muslim 40.6840: Abu Hurairah

The Prophet ﷺ said: "Two are the types among the denizens of the Fire, someone possessing whips - like the tail of an ox - who flogs people with them - and the second is the women who are naked despite being dressed, and who are seduced [to wrong paths] and seduce others with their hair high like humps. These women will not get into the Garden and they will not even perceive the fragrance of the Garden, although it can be perceived from very far away."

246. Makers of pictures will be commanded to give them life.
Muslim 24.5266: A'ishah

I bought a carpet with pictures for the Prophet ﷺ; but when he saw it, he stayed at the door and did not come in. Perceiving signs of distaste upon his face, I said: "the Messenger of Allah, I repent to Allah and His Messenger, but tell me what is the wrong action that I have committed." Thereupon he asked: "What is this carpet?" I replied: "I bought it for you so that you might sit on it and rest." He retorted: "The people who made these pictures will be tormented and asked to bring to life what they tried to create." He added: "Angels do not enter a house in which there is a picture."

247. Well advising but ill practising people are in the Fire.
Bukhari 4.489: Abu Wa'il

The Prophet ﷺ is reported to have said: "A man will be brought on the Day of Rising and thrown in the Fire, so that his intestines will come out, and he will go around like a donkey walking around a millstone. The people of the Fire will gather around him and say: 'So and so! you used to order us to do good deeds and forbid us to do bad deeds, what is wrong with you?' He will reply: 'Yes, I used to order you to do good deeds, but I did not do them myself, and I used to forbid you to do bad deeds, but I myself used to do them.'"

248. The Garden for spreading salaam, sadaqah and for salat.
Mishkat: Tirmidhi/Abu Yusuf 'Abdullah ibn Salam

'Abdullah heard the Prophet ﷺ say: "O people! Spread [the greeting of] salaam, feed the poor and needy, behave kindly to your blood relations, offer salat when others are asleep, and thus enter the Garden in peace."

249. The Garden for memorising Allah's ninety-nine names.
Muslim 35.6475: Abu Hurairah

The Prophet ﷺ once said: "Allah has ninety-nine names; whoever commits them to memory will enter the Garden... ."

250. Blessings on the Prophet ﷺ draw one close to him.
Mishkat: Tirmidhi/Ibn Mas'ud

The Prophet ﷺ said: "The one closest to me on the Day of Rising will be someone who invokes the greatest number of blessings upon me."

251. Abu Bakr combined several deeds in a day.
Muslim 31.5880: Abu Hurairah

The Prophet ﷺ once asked his companions: "Who among you is fasting today?" Abu Bakr said: "I am." He continued: "Who followed a bier today?" Abu Bakr said: "I did." He again said: "Who has served food to the needy?" Abu Bakr said: "I have." He asked: "Who has visited a sick person today?" Abu Bakr said: "I." Thereupon he concluded: "He must enter the Garden who combines in himself all these."

252. Fasting while on jihad, a ditch between one and the Fire. *Mishkat*: Tirmidhi/Abu Umamah

The Prophet ﷺ said: "If anyone fasts for a day while on jihad, Allah will put between him and the Fire a ditch as wide as the distance between Heaven and Earth."

253. Specific doors to the Garden.
Muslim 5.2239: Abu Hurairah

The Prophet ﷺ once said: " Those who engage in salat will be invited to enter the Garden by the gate of salat; those who take part in jihad will be invited to enter by the gate of jihad; those who give sadaqah will be invited to enter by the gate of sadaqah; and those who observe fast will be invited to enter by the gate of ar-Rayyan." Abu Bakr asked: "Will anyone be invited to enter by all those gates?" The Prophet ﷺ said: "Yes, and I hope you will be one of them."

254. Impatient people might go to the Fire.
Bukhari 9.176: Ibn Abbas

The Prophet ﷺ said: "Whoever disapproves of something done by his ruler should be patient, for whoever disobeys the [right-acting] ruler even a little will die as those who died in the time of jahiliyyah.

255. Patient blind people are rewarded with the Garden.
Bukhari 7.557: Anas ibn Malik

I heard the Messenger of Allah ﷺ saying, "Allah says: 'If I deprive my slave of his two beloved things [i.e., his eyes] and he remains patient, I will let him enter the Garden in compensation for them.'"

256. The seven to be in Allah's shade on that Day.
Muslim 5.2248: Abu Hurairah

The Prophet ﷺ said: "Seven are the people whom Allah will protect with His shade on the Day of Judgement, when there will be no shade but His: [1] a just ruler, [2] a youth who grew up in worship, [3] a person whose heart is attached to the mosques, [4] a person who loves and meets another and separates from him for the sake of Allah, [5] a man whom a beautiful woman of high rank attempts to seduce but who rejects the offer, saying 'I fear Allah,' [6] a person who gives sadaqah, concealing it so that the right hand does not know what the left has given, and [7] a person who remembers Allah in secret so much so that his eyes shed tears."

257. Merit of guiding others to Islam.
Muslim 31.5918: Sahl ibn Sa'd

While preparing the expedition of Khaybar, the Prophet ﷺ chose 'Ali ibn Abi Talib to hold the banner, advising him thus: "Advance cautiously until you reach their open places, thereafter invite them to Islam and tell them what is obligatory for them from the rights of Allah; for, by Allah, if Allah guides even one person by means of you to Himself, that is better for you than to possess the most valuable camels [or any other worldly wealth]."

SUMMARY

Reviewing the hadith in general brings the indescribable pleasure of feeling as if one were in the company of the Prophet ﷺ and his honourable companions. It contributes greatly to increasing one's iman, as pondering the hadith highlights the power of Almighty Allah and the authenticity of the Prophet's mission. Specifically, this hadith compilation chiefly aims to draw the readers' attention towards death and the Day of Judgement and help them strive for safety from the Fire and admission to the Garden. The essence of the compilation suggests that the ultimate provisions for admission to the Garden come down to two elements: iman in Allah and sound social behaviour. Let us demonstrate this by closely examining each element of the equation.

To start with, we need to remember that Allah's forgiveness is the determining factor for admission to the Garden; deeds alone, no matter how great, cannot suffice. The Prophet ﷺ explained to his companions that not even he could enter the Garden for any reason other than "Allah wrapping him in His mercy." This is why the first term of the equation requires a modifier with the word the Garden.

But why is the second term composed of only two elements, iman and social behaviour? What about the essential duties such as salat, which is "the first thing about which people will be called to account" in the Judgement process? What about special deeds, like jihad, which are known to take one directly to the Garden?

The response is twofold. In the first place, it is well known that the Judgement process considers both positive and negative deeds, making a balance between them. If a middle course is taken, the pool of ordinary good deeds is likely to compensate for the pool of ordinary bad deeds, especially considering the generosity of the Judge. After that simplification, however, there will remain special elements that cannot be annulled even by the best possible deeds: these are disbelief and unlawful social behaviour. That disbelief is unforgivable is a truism and thus dispenses with explanations. As for social behaviour, the hadith explain breathtakingly that (1) jihad can clear all the wrong actions of a person except what is due to other people, such as debts; (2) one may become bankrupt for having harmed other people, whose accounts will be credited from one's account in compensation for the harm caused; and (3) in cases of mutual offences, even if both parts are quit with Allah, their entrance to the Garden will still be delayed until they settle their disagreement. The wisdom in emphasizing social behaviour is understandable. The essence of Islam - as the very word Islam itself proclaims - is peaceful community life under the authority of One Lord, and such a community life is simply impossible without mutual respect and good dealings among the members of society.

In the second place, real iman and sound social behaviour encompass the entire body of Islamic deeds. Having faith in Allah requires understanding, accepting, and implementing all the duties that He has ordained, starting with the basics (declaration of that iman, salat, zakat, fast, hajj) and expanding to extra deeds, which bring one "closer to Him." In fact, abandoning certain deeds, like salat, simply equals "disbelief." It is also only through real iman that special deeds like jihad can be achieved; sacrificing one's own life for the sake of Allah is impossible for a person whose iman is weak. Furthermore, real faith forbids all that Allah has forbidden, including unlawful killing, adultery, greediness, and pride. Equally, sound social behaviour implies various acts toward family members, neighbours, and society as a whole. The hadith explain, among other things, that (1) children's behaviour toward their parents is for them a ticket to the Garden or the Fire, (2) a mother will be admitted to the Garden for having deprived herself to feed her daughters, (3) the wife who pleases her husband will be admitted to the Garden, (4) "the best of men are those who behave best toward their wives," (5) the person "whose neighbour is not secure from his or her wrongful conduct will not enter the Garden," and (6) "putting things right between people is better than fasting, praying, and sadaqah."

In fact, iman and social behaviour are naturally combined. The Prophet ﷺ explained that "none has iman till he wishes for his Muslim brother what he desires for himself," thereby confirming Allah's own words, "Son of Adam, I was sick but you did not visit Me," He indicates that a believer should see in another believer the representative of his Almighty Creator.

As well as teaching the above creed in theory, the Messenger of Allah ﷺ set a practical example through his own lifestyle, showing that the combination of iman and sound social behaviour makes the Muslim both active in worship and humble. It makes him steadfast in prayer not only to fulfil a prescribed duty, but also to express gratitude to Allah. It also deters his mind from virtually all the pleasures and wealth of this world. If he were to be given a mountain of gold, "in three days he would spend it all for the sake of Allah," except what he needs "to pay his debts," to fulfil other people's rights over him.

In turn, the companions of the Prophet ﷺ perpetuated this good example, questioning their own faith and combining all sorts of good deeds to improve that faith and credit their accounts. On a single day, they would be "observing the fast, following the bier, feeding the needy, visiting the sick," and so forth. They would never hurt other people, let alone violate their rights. Rather, they would place other people's rights above their own rights. Even at the time of dying they would remember that "a living person has more right to wear new clothes than a dead one" and thus make a will to be shrouded in worn-out clothes.

The road to salvation has therefore been paved by the Prophet ﷺ and the generations that followed him. It is up to the current and future generations to follow in their footsteps by strengthening their faith and maintaining sound social behaviour.